Time Management, Planning, and Prioritization for Librarians

Judith A. Siess

The Scarecrow Press, Inc.
Lanham, Maryland, and Oxford
2002

SCARECROW PRESS, INC.

Published in the United States of America
by Scarecrow Press, Inc.
A wholly owned subsidiary of
The Rowman & Littlefield Publishing Group, Inc.
4501 Forbes Boulevard, Suite 200, Lanham, Maryland 20706
www.scarecrowpress.com

12 Hid's Copse Road
Cumnor Hill, Oxford OX2 9JJ, England

British Library Cataloguing in Publication Information Available

Library of Congress Cataloging-in-Publication Data Available

ISBN 0-8108-4438-9 (pbk. : alk. paper)

♾™ The paper used in this publication meets the minimum requirements of
American National Standard for Information Sciences—Permanence of
Paper for Printed Library Materials, ANSI/NISO Z39.48-1992.
Manufactured in the United States of America.

Contents

Acknowledgments

First and foremost, I have to thank my husband, Steve Bremseth, for his patience and willingness to do without me while I was researching and writing this book. I also owe him for his support and understanding in everything I do. He is my rock.

Michelle Sutton-Kerchner edited my second book, *The OPL Sourcebook*, and did such a superb job of *not* changing my rather unique style that I hired her to ready this book for publication. For allowing me to concentrate on content rather than form, I am extremely grateful.

Finally, I want to thank Sue Easun, acquisitions editor for Scarecrow Press, for crossing that aisle at the exhibits at SLA 2000 and asking me to write this book. I would never have thought of it on my own. I hope this book lives up to her expectations.

Preface

As has been the case for many of my colleagues, librarianship has been a second career for me. However, I think I always wanted to be a librarian. After college and graduate school (resulting in interesting but relatively useless degrees in anthropology), I finally went to library school. I had worked in libraries in grade school and junior high, and I had done term papers in high school and college using the great collection of the University of Illinois. I even had run a couple of small corporate libraries (and didn't do a bad job at all, looking back on it). Now I had a chance to get a formal library education at the University of Illinois at Urbana-Champaign.

I thoroughly enjoyed library school. I even did a thesis, which was not required (or even encouraged). I did an internship under the late Martha Blake at the U.S. Army Corps of Engineers Construction Engineering Research Laboratory. The internship was not required either, but it was there that I learned much of what I know about customer service and relationship-building. At the time I was working for the University of Illinois, running the Agricultural Economics Reference Room. It was like having my own private laboratory. As I learned to do things in class, I put them into practice. We had online searching, a primitive online catalog (remember, this was 1980–1982), and even e-mail.

My first professional job was starting a library for a small biotechnology research and development firm in rural Ohio. I didn't know anything about enzymes (the area in which the company was doing research), but I knew enough to ask questions. Before I left for my final interview, I asked the librarians at the chemistry and biology libraries at the University of Illinois for a list of books and journals that they considered essential. Library services and use increased as the company grew from 15 to 40 employees. Unfortunately, after a few years the company began to go downhill and I was laid off. (I take pride that I was neither the first employee hired nor the last let go.)

My husband's new job took us to Cleveland, Ohio. I had a succession of short-term jobs; one was for another biotech startup company, then two jobs subbing for librarians on maternity leave. Finally I found the "perfect" job. I became the engineering librarian at Bailey Controls Company (now a part of ABB Automation). I was the only information professional working in what became a US$2 billion global firm, with over 16,000 employees. Over time, the library changed from the Engineering Library to the Corporate Information and Research Center.

However, I eventually tired of trying to make sense of an increasingly bureaucratic organization and of trying to implement current information practices (especially knowledge management) in a company historically unwilling to share information between departments. As I approached my 50th birthday and its attendant mid-life crisis, I decided this was not what I wanted to be doing. So I left Bailey to start my own business, Information Bridges International, Inc. IBI's primary business is publishing *The One-Person Library: A Newsletter for Librarians and Management,* which I purchased in 1998 from its founder, Guy St. Clair. I also enjoy traveling the world presenting workshops on small library management and, of course, time management.

I have always been active in library professional associations, dating back to library school and the excellent example set by Linda C. Smith, who remains one of my best advisors. I am extremely proud of having been the first chair of the Solo Librarians Division of the Special Libraries Association. I have gained a great deal of experience and satisfaction by serving on local, divisional, and national committees and boards. I also make it a point to go back to my alma mater about once a year (and anywhere else that invites me) to tell library school students what life is like in the "real world." The library profession has been good to me, and I feel it is vital to give back to it. This brings me to why I wrote this book. In my work with solo or one-person librarians (OPLs), the question that comes up most often is, "How can I do it all?" It took me a while to come up with the answer: "You don't do it all!" That led me to develop a workshop on *time management.* Time management inevitably led to prioritization, and prioritization led to strategic planning. You cannot decide which tasks to do without knowing which are most important—*prioritization*. And you cannot prioritize unless you know where you are going—*strategic planning*. Therefore, one cannot address time management without the other two parts of the process.

Of course, the first thing I did when planning the time management workshop was to search the literature. I found loads of books on time management but only four on time management for librarians. One of these was for public librarians; one was for school librarians; and all were written in the early 1990s. Therefore, I had to develop the workshop based on generalities and my personal experience.

How this got to be a book is an interesting story. Aspiring authors have asked me, "How do I find a publisher?" I am the wrong person to ask. When I was writing my first book, *The SOLO Librarian's Sourcebook*, I just walked up to Tom Hogan, Sr., president of Information Today, Inc., at an SLA conference and said, "I'm writing a book. Do you want to publish it?" He said, "Okay," and I had my first publisher. This book came about in an even easier way. I was exhibiting at another SLA conference. Across the way was the Scarecrow Press booth. Acquisitions editor Sue Easun saw the speaker's ribbon on my badge and asked, "What did you speak about?" When I told her I had presented a workshop on time management, planning, and prioritization for solo librarians, she said, "Would you be interested in writing a book about that for Scarecrow?" Obviously, I said yes, and this book is the result.

I thought a book just for OPLs would have a very limited audience, and since time management is a problem for all librarians, I expanded the scope to include all special librarians. Why just *special* librarians? I have never worked in a public or school library (except way back in junior high school). My work experience has been only in special libraries—in academia, government, and corporate settings. (Okay, I have never worked in a law or medical library either, but because they are similar enough to corporate libraries, after some additional research, I feel comfortable talking about them.)

I suppose you are wondering if I practice all the techniques in this book. Of course not! I'm sure you've heard the saying, "Those who can, do; those who cannot, teach." Well, it's not quite that bad. But this is a "Do as I say, not as I do" book. Why? I am a one-person company, answerable only to myself, and so I do not have to adhere to anyone's timetable or priorities but my own. However—and this is very important—no matter how much I may procrastinate, I get everything done on time. And that's what is really important. When one of my students asked me if I had written a strategic plan, I replied, "No, but since I am answerable to no one else—not even for funding—it is perfectly fine to have it only in my head." Unfortunately, this is no excuse for you to do the same.

Andrew Berner, library director and curator of collections at the University Club in New York and co-founder of *The One-Person Library: A Newsletter for Librarians and Management*, wrote about time management for my first book, *The SOLO Librarian's Sourcebook*.

Here is some of what he wrote about the three Ps of effective time management: planning, prioritization, and procrastination (Berner in Siess):

> If ever there was a group for whom time management is an important concept, it's solo librarians. With so much to do and, generally, no one to whom work can be delegated, it becomes essential that the solo librarian be aware of the basic principles of good time management. Too often, however, the librarian seeks time management "tricks," things that will enable a job to be done more quickly. In other words, they seek efficiency, where in fact they should be seeking effectiveness. Time management is not just looking for ways to cut down on the time it takes to do specific tasks (though that certainly can be a part of it). To be sure, there is much more to time management than simply being aware of the importance of planning, priorities and procrastination. Much can—and has—been written on each of them, as well as on the many other aspects of good time management. Still, these are three powerful tools (two to use and one to avoid) in any solo librarian's arsenal of time management weapons. A knowledge of them can be used to help the librarian function not only in a more efficient manner, but—even more important—in a more effective manner as well. And after all, that's what being a one-person librarian is all about.

What Berner wrote is true even for non-solo librarians. I know of very few special librarians who have all the help, all the money, and all the time they want or need. So much for the preliminaries, now on to the main event.

1
How Do You Look at Time?

To manage time well, one must have a good perception of time (Cochran, 7).

Time, which once seemed free and elastic, has grown elusive and tight, and our measure of its worth is changing dramatically (Mackenzie, 13).

... time simply exists. It's not out to get you (Tullier, 58).

Before you can begin to manage time, you have to understand it. Nearly everyone writing about time management has said something about the fundamental nature of time.

Time is a continuum ... in which events succeed one another from past through present to future (*Webster's* Dictionary in Nutty).

We cannot save time; we can only spend it (Cochran, 10).

Parkinson's Law, or the Rising Pyramid: Work expands so as to fill the time available for its completion (Parkinson, 2).

Money comes and goes—Time just goes (Davidson, The Complete Idiot's Guide® to Managing Your Time, 69).

Time poses this dilemma: We never have enough of it, but we have all there is (Weeks, 4).

You can always get more stuff, and you can always get more money. But you can't get more time (Jasper, 15).

We are all given a finite amount of time, but the irony is that we never know how much we have until it's all gone (LeBoeuf, 9–10).

It is because we have so much time that we squander it (Koch, 149).

Think of your time as money and invest it wisely every day (Porat, 79).

To sum up all of this: Time is democratic—we all have the same amount of time. Time is perishable. Time is a nonrenewable resource. Time is even more valuable than money, because one can always get more money; however, once time is spent, it cannot be replaced.

Because of the nature of time, the nature of the modern world, and the nature of librarianship, most librarians feel under constant pressure—pressure to save time, to manage time, to make the best use of our time. Adding to these general time pressures is the ever-increasing availability of technology. New tools are always being touted as being the ultimate time-management tool, such as computers, cellular phones, pagers, and personal digital assistants (PDAs). And who knows what more lies in the future?

As if these pressures are not enough, there is the constant pressure from business and financial constraints. Virtually every library—whether in the private, not-for-profit, academic, medical, legal, or any other sector——has had to face either downsizing or a decreased budget, if not in the library itself then in its parent organization. "Clerical tasks have been pushed up in organizations, which is not necessarily a good thing" (Mark Ellwood in Abernathy, 22). One company I worked for cut costs by eliminating many of the secretaries. This left engineers, who were paid many times as much as the secretaries, writing their own letters, doing their own photocopying, and so on. Not only did this cost the company more money, but the quality of the work suffered (not to mention morale). The same thing has happened in many libraries. Clerical support has been cut or even eliminated. Tasks that were done by low-paid nonprofessionals are now done by higher-paid librarians. This necessary, but lower-priority, work takes up the time available for the important, value-added work that only the librarians can do. The organization suffers from loss of information; the library suffers from loss of status; and the librarians suffer from loss of morale. Who benefits? Only the bottom line and that, too, will suffer eventually.

Therefore, today it is more important than ever for librarians to manage their time and their priorities—keeping themselves on track for maximum value to their organizations. "By not managing your time, you deny yourself the opportunity to do outstanding work" (Mackenzie, 10).

You must remember, however, that you do not really manage time—you manage *your* use of time. A university business librarian said, "It's my opinion now that the phrase 'time management' is an oxymoron. No one has any more time than anyone else because time is a given. There are 60 minutes in an hour; 24 hrs in a day. No one has any more or any less of that. So I cannot control the amount of time that I have; the only thing I can control are my commitments." Anne Marie Turner says,

> To talk about time as being organized or managed is a misnomer. Time is already organized. It is counted in precisely the same orderly increments the world over. You can, however, manage your own use of time. Learn to use the clock as a tool. Negotiate the demands of an ever-changing schedule. Understand how to modify language, attitude, and behavior to keep time from slipping away from you forevermore.

Here are 25 myths and the corresponding truths about time:

1. *Myth:* Time can be managed. *Truth:* You manage activities, not time.
2. *Myth:* The longer or harder you work, the more you accomplish. *Truth:* It is better to work effectively. The law of diminishing returns applies here (especially after 48 hours a week).
3. *Myth:* If you want something done right, do it yourself. *Truth:* Delegating is good if done properly, and for most of us delegating is necessary.
4. *Myth:* You are not supposed to enjoy work. *Truth:* If you do not enjoy what you are doing, you will become frustrated and feel as if you are always behind.
5. *Myth:* We should take pride in working hard. *Truth:* Librarians should take pride in working smart.
6. *Myth:* You should try to do the most in the least amount of time. *Truth:* It is better to do it right.
7. *Myth:* Technology will help you do it better and faster. *Truth:* Technology can speed up routine tasks but not creative work. Technology often also makes things more complicated.
8. *Myth:* Do one thing at a time. *Truth:* Use your multilevel, multitasking abilities.
9. *Myth:* Get more done, and you will be happier. *Truth:* No, you will just get more done.

10. *Myth:* Time management takes away your freedom—and I am a spontaneous sort of person. *Truth:* True freedom comes through discipline.
11. *Myth:* I do not have time to do time management. *Truth:* You do not have time *not* to.
12. *Myth:* I am doing well at my job, so I must be managing my time just fine. *Truth:* But you could be doing it better.
13. *Myth:* I work better under pressure; time management would take away that edge. *Truth:* Nobody works better under pressure. It is just an excuse for procrastination.
14. *Myth:* An empty in-box is the goal. *Truth:* You do not need to and should not do everything. Do high-priority items first.
15. *Myth:* Follow routines to get more done. *Truth:* Follow your passion. Live your joy!
16. *Myth:* Productive people work harder than others. *Truth:* When you are in control, you are relaxed.
17. *Myth:* There are many ways to save time. *Truth:* You cannot save time, only spend it; however, you can improve how you spend it.
18. *Myth:* No one ever has enough time. *Truth:* We all have as much time as there is.
19. *Myth:* You can make up for lost time. *Truth:* Once a moment is lost, it is lost forever.
20. *Myth:* I do not have the time. *Truth:* If you think the task is important enough, you will find the time.
21. *Myth:* Activity means productivity. *Truth:* Activity means activity, nothing more. Productivity is doing the right things and sometimes may mean no action at all.
22. *Myth:* Efficiency means effectiveness. *Truth: Efficiency* is doing things right; *effectiveness* is doing the right things.
23. *Myth:* Results are proportionate to the time spent. *Truth:* Results are proportionate to the time well spent.
24. *Myth:* The easy way is the best way. *Truth:* Sometimes. Being lazy is often the key to efficiency.
25. *Myth:* There is only one best way. *Truth:* No, each person must find his or her own best way.

> **QUIZ: How Do You Look at Time?**
>
> - List two things you want to do but never have the time for.
> - List one thing you do but want to stop doing.
> - If I had more time I would_____. (Finish the sentence.)
> - List something you resent having to do but continue to do just to please someone else.
> - List something you do just because "It has always been done."
> - List things you have said yes to but now wish you had said no to.

Not only do people not understand the true nature of time, they also interact with time in different ways. Eisenberg (12–15) describes 10 different time styles:

1. The self-interrupter, who is distracted easily.
2. The time waster who, among other things, spends a lot of time chatting with co-workers.
3. The tardy one, who is never on time and does not plan ahead.
4. The crisis manager, who leaves everything to the last minute.
5. The scattered person, who often loses track of details.
6. The procrastinator. We all know one of these.
7. The undirected or indecisive person, who has not set his or her priorities.
8. The juggler, who multitasks well.
9. The obsessively organized worker, who overdoes a good thing and drives others nuts and who believes in organization for the sake of organization.
10. The efficient one, who does everything right.

I would wager that every organization has at least one employee fitting each of the categories above. The problem comes in when one of the first nine categories fits the librarian or, even worse, the librarian's boss.

There are other ways of describing how people look at and use time. One is right-brained versus left-brained. Take the quiz in the box below to see which you are.

QUIZ: Left-Brained or Right-Brained (adapted from Silber).

1. Are you always on time or early for appointments?
2. Does planning make you feel secure rather than trapped?
3. Are interruptions annoying to you, rather than exciting?
4. Do you always have a written to-do list?
5. Do you think daydreaming is a waste of time?
6. Do you seldom do anything based on instinct or impulse?
7. Do you nearly always read the instructions completely before using a new piece of equipment or software?
8. Do you nearly always wear a watch?
9. Do you prefer written directions to a map?
10. Is your checkbook always balanced to the penny?
11. Do you pay your credit card bills off in full every month?
12. Do you always follow rules even when you disagree with them?
13. Do you get right to the point when telling a story?
14. Do you prefer to minimize risks in life?
15. Do you have all the paperwork for your taxes in hand before you start?
16. Do you make a to-do list for weekend errands?
17. Do you make an itinerary for business trips?
18. Do you make an itinerary for *personal* trips, too?
19. Do you seldom change your mind once a decision is made?
20. Do you think change is frightening rather than exciting?
21. Do you bring back office supplies rather than toys from conferences?
22. Do you file paper rather than pile it?
23. Are you often asked to serve on planning committees?
24. In your office, does everything have a place and is everything in its place?
25. Do you already have things planned for next year, and the year after?
26. Would people *never* describe you as a free spirit?
27. Do you prefer to work on one thing at a time?
28. In personnel matters, do you prefer to write a memo rather than confront someone?
29. Do you read the newspaper in sequential order?

30. Do you nearly always think before you speak?

Having more than 20 "yes" answers indicates that you are a logical, left-brained thinker. Having more than 20 "no" answers means that you lean toward creative, right-brained thinking. Anything else means you have characteristics of both.

Right-brained people are artistic, creative, visual, emotional, intuitive, nonlinear, persuasive, unpredictable, dramatic, and spontaneous; they have good mathematical ability, look at things spatially, see the big picture, and are good at multitasking. Left-brained people are detail-oriented, the timekeepers, logical, analytical, linear, judgmental, verbal, compartmentalized, good at researching, tidy, organized, compulsive, perfectionist, punctual, cautious, controlling, and focused; they learn patterns well, follow directions, separate work from play, dislike change, and act as the "voice of reason."

Similar to right-brained versus left-brain typing is the monochronic/polychronic dichotomy. The monochronic person does one thing at a time, concentrates on the job, is always on time, is committed to the job, follows plans religiously, and has short-term relationships (McGee-Cooper, 28). The polychronic person can do many things at once, does not mind being interrupted, *tries* to be on time, is committed to people, changes plans often and easily, and has lifetime relationships. Business is monochronic. Fortunately, "mothers are polychronic by necessity" (McGee-Cooper, 32).

Still another way to think about time is divergent versus convergent. Divergent thinkers expand, see the big picture, skip around, do it now, and look for multiple answers; they are intuitive, comfortable with ambiguity, or "scatter-brained." Convergent thinkers contract, zero in, go step-by-step, plan for later, prefer hard data, and look for the right answer; they are patient, logical, or "narrow-minded." "People with divergent minds can create 10 times as many tasks as they and their colleagues combined can complete" (McGee-Cooper, 103). Haven't we all had a boss like that?

As you can see, right-brained, polychronic, and divergent are all names for the same basic personality. McGee-Cooper (102–103) says:

The divergent mind is great at generating quantity [such as tasks], but it has a difficult time remembering what has been generated. It needs a system for seeing all of the tasks that have been identified and their relative importance to one another. If there is no system in place for this 'big picturing' to happen, right-brained people will just get started on the last item on the list and forget about important ongoing projects that were created two weeks ago.

Left-brained, monochronic, and convergent also describe the same basic personality type. Obviously, the best situation would be to be a combination of all the best of both personalities, but most of us are mostly one or the other. I am almost completely a left-brained, monochronic, convergent thinker. However, I also look at things spatially, am a great multitasker, have lifetime relationships, and want to do things immediately—all traits of the opposite personality. (Of course, I am married to a right-brained, polychronic, divergent person. It always seems to happen that way. The same is often true of boss and employee—unfortunately.)

Traditional time-management products and techniques are designed for the left-brained person and may not be suited for the right-brained person. They focus on increasing productivity but ignore innovation and creativity. They ignore polychronic time. They view daydreaming as unfocused and wasteful. They measure only tangible results. They assume everything can be solved and dealt with logically (McGee-Cooper, 83–84).

What happens if you are a right-brained or creative person? How should you deal with time? Silber's book is just for you, but first let's get some myths out of the way (4–5):

- *Myth:* You have unlimited energy. *Truth:* No one does; you still need to manage your time.
- *Myth:* You are lazy. *Truth:* No, when you appear not to be working you are probably thinking or planning.
- *Myth:* You fail to follow through. *Truth:* You are just easily distracted by new ideas.
- *Myth:* You are irresponsible. *Truth:* Your priorities may be different from those of other people.
- *Myth:* You hate structure. *Truth:* You may have a higher tolerance for freedom, but chaos is not creative.
- *Myth:* You are impulsive. *Truth:* You can learn to stop and think.

Creative persons need to adapt the techniques in this and other time-management books to their particular time-style and personality. Use your creative abilities to find methods that you feel comfortable with and that work for you. Most likely, you will also have to work harder at time management and allow more time to change poor time-management habits. But you *will* succeed.

Now that you have figured out how you look at time, you will need to decide how your library and organization look at and value time. Do you usually work only the typical 40 hours a week (or 35, or whatever), or are you expected to work overtime? How much overtime? Are you expected to come in on time or punch a time clock, or can you set your own schedule? Is speed more important than quality? Is everything a rush or a crisis? How well you do may depend on how well your ideas of time fit in with the library or organization. If it is not a good fit, then you may want to look at other opportunities.

QUIZ: Time Habits (adapted from Porat and Ferner).

1. Do you delegate enough (and not just the easy stuff)?
2. Do you keep unneeded information and publications from taking up your time?
3. When in doubt, do you throw it out?
4. Do you make minor decisions quickly?
5. Do you set deadlines?
6. Do you take time to plan?
7. Do you always have something to work on when waiting?
8. Do you avoid rehashing old mistakes?
9. Do you control time, or does it control you?
10. Do you plan free time for whatever you want to do?
11. Are you spending your time the way you really want to?
12. Do you feel harried and obligated to do too many things you really do not want to do?
13. Do you get a feeling of self-satisfaction and accomplishment from your work?
14. Do you take work home?
15. Can you manage the stress in your work?
16. Do you seldom feel tense and insecure?
17. Do you have seldom have guilty feelings about not doing a better job?
18. Is your job fun?
19. Are you giving your family as much time as you (and they) would like?
20. Do you have time to keep physically fit?
21. Do you take all of your vacation time?

> The more "no" answers you have, the more you need to change the way you handle and manage your time. Read on.

Pareto and the 80/20 Principle

Doing more things faster is no substitute for doing the right things.

A. Roger Merrill

Vilfredo Pareto (1848–1923) was an Italian economist who examined patterns of wealth and income in nineteenth-century England. He found that the distribution was predictably unbalanced. He also found that this was true in earlier times and in other countries. After further study, Pareto estimated that 80 percent of the world's most important tasks are accomplished in 20 percent of the available time. "The significance of the 80/20 Principle lay dormant for a generation" [until the 1940s] (Koch, 7). Since then, "80/20 has become shorthand for [an] unbalanced relationship, whether or not the precise result is 80/20" (Koch, 30). Since Pareto, the 80/20 Principle has been found to apply, more or less, to almost everything. Koch (3) adds, "The 80/20 Principle can and should be used by every intelligent person in their daily life, by every social grouping and form of society. It can help individuals and groups achieve much more, with much less effort." You will find references to this concept all through the time-management literature and in this book as well.

The Pareto Principle is somewhat related to another principle, one that librarians are more familiar with—Zipf's Principle of Least Effort. George K. Zipf, a professor of philology at Harvard University, discovered that resources tend to arrange themselves to minimize work. From 20 to 30 percent of a resource accounts for 70 to 80 percent of its related activity (Koch, 7).

Time Wasters

Following the Pareto Principle, librarians must strive always to use 80 percent of their time on the 20 percent of the tasks that are most important. That means trying not to waste time. We all waste time—it is inevitable. No one is 100 percent effective 100 percent of the time. It is important to learn how we waste time in our work lives, and then work toward eliminating as many of the time-wasting behaviors as possible. What *is* a time waster? Ferner (12) says that a time-management problem is "activities that are taking up large amounts of time without corresponding value." I have divided time wasters into eight categories: personal, other people, machines, methods and procedures, procrastination, management, planning, and communication. Most categories, in turn, can be divided into *internal time wasters* (things we can control or change) and *external time wasters* (caused by someone else and not controllable). Let's look at each category in turn.

1. **Personal.** *Internal:* the inability to say no, perfectionism, a lack of priorities, negative emotions (such as guilt, anger, fear, worry), negative thinking, a poor attitude, indecision, personal disorganization, duplication of effort, confused responsibility and authority, mistakes or ineffective performance, fatigue, lack of concentration, inconsistency, lack of discipline, a cluttered workspace, taking over others' jobs or projects, being ill-prepared for a call or meeting, rationalizing or making excuses, wasting your most productive hours of the day, having too many personal or outside activities, blaming others, complaining, daydreaming, trying to be an expert when you are not, spreading yourself too thin, making unrealistic promises, attempting too much, not getting feedback from others, hearing only what you want to hear, not listening, socializing and interoffice travel to see what is going on or to gossip. *External:* none.

2. **Other People.** *Internal:* responding to crises or fire-fighting, micromanaging assistants, excessive socializing. *External:* interruptions, walk-in salespersons, people late for appointments, visitors, the office pest, others who procrastinate, a disorganized boss, mistakes of others, busy work, meetings, low morale, waiting for answers, dealing with personal problems of others, waiting in general ("You spend seven years of your life waiting!" [Corcoran, 117]).

3. **Machines.** *Internal:* looking up phone and fax numbers, looking up e-mail addresses or URLs (uniform resource locators), playing phone tag, getting incomplete phone messages, learning or upgrading software, equipment failure owing to a lack of preventive maintenance, failure to backup computer files. *External:* the telephone, the computer, not enough office equipment, so-called free software ("free" is not better if it takes more time).

4. **Methods and Procedures.** *Internal*: slavishly following rules, falling into a routine, making poor time estimates, running to your boss or a colleague with each question you have, standing in line to make one copy, dealing with red tape, getting too many people involved on a project or committee, decision-making without proper research, monotasking, continuing to do some or all of what you used to do after a promotion or getting new responsibilities, returning all phone messages yourself, working in clutter, handling paper without making a decision about it, not reading efficiently, not having procedures, not delegating or outsourcing, not noting changed priorities, not evaluating your failures, not reusing what you have already done (reinventing the wheel), not using the ideas of others, not requesting or responding to feedback, not maintaining paper and electronic files, not using tickler files or reminder notes, not having standards or progress reports, not confirming appointments, not using commuter or waiting time. *External:* looking for people or equipment, a poor office layout, poor filing systems, inadequate staff, traveling.

5. **Procrastination.** *Internal:* waiting until the last minute, waiting for the so-called right time, putting off an unpleasant job, doing it yourself rather than teaching someone else to do it, leaving tasks unfinished, underestimating how long a job will take, taking back a job you delegated. *External*: none.

6. **Management.** *Internal*: managing by crisis, fire-fighting, letting your boss micromanage you, micromanaging others, overscheduling yourself, becoming overly involved in routine details, not managing conflict, not coping with change, having unclear goals, making snap decisions. *External*: the mail, dealing with multiple bosses, waiting for instructions from others, always having to sign or approve everything, dealing with red tape, having no authority, having poor working conditions (such as inadequate lighting and excessive noise), having unclear job descriptions ("We just don't know what we are expected to do." [Stanley Smith, 37]).

7. **Planning.** *Internal:* not planning, not having a daily plan, not following your goals, taking a goal for granted, looking too far ahead of your goal, doing too much planning and taking too little action, doing all the planning yourself, complaining when your plan is not working, having priorities that are unclear or that change, having no self-imposed deadlines. *External:* changing goals by management, lack of support by colleagues or management, failure of funding.

8. **Communication.** *Internal:* writing when you should call—and vice versa, communicating with everyone the same way, not an-

swering questions fully, and using words people do not understand, writing long letters, not listening, having incomplete information. *External:* none.

As you can see, I think that most time wasters are internal, that is, they can—and must—be controlled. We all have the power to improve our time management skills. All we need are the tools. For these, see the next section.

How does all this relate to librarians? "Research into the time management practices of librarians indicates that many share common problems, regardless of the type of library in which they work" (Cochran, 4). Based on various studies, including those of Gothberg and Cochran, here are the librarian's top 10 time wasters:

1. Meetings. According to Gothberg, special library managers spend less time in meetings...than managers of other types of libraries. *Both internal and external.*
2. The telephone. "The biggest single time waster, worldwide, is telephone interruptions" (Mackenzie, 7). *Internal and external.*
3. Drop-in visitors. *Internal and external.*
4. Inaccurate, inadequate, or delayed information. *External.*
5. Attempting too much or having unrealistic time estimates. *Internal.*
6. Crises generated by you or your staff. *Mostly external.*
7. An inability to say no. *Internal.*
8. Indecision, procrastination. *Internal.*
9. Lack of self-discipline. *Internal.*
10. Leaving tasks unfinished. *Internal.*

Other time wasters mentioned by at least one writer are (in no particular order): *Internal:* too much time spent on routine tasks and a lack of methods and procedures handling them; *External:* establishing priorities, failing to keep accurate and accessible records, running unnecessary errands, looking for keys, running out of supplies, role conflicts, technology, inadequate staff (especially for one-person or solo librarians), barriers from the organizational culture, computers, user instructions, and last—but certainly not least—Intranets, the Internet, and e-mail.

Stop Wasting Time

Don't you wish that you could just say, "I'm not going to waste any more time"? But of course it is not that easy. You have been wasting time for a long while, and it has become a habit. Habits are difficult to break. First you must admit that there is a problem. You have already done that just by reading this book. Then you need to identify how you waste time. Go back over the preceding section and see which time wasters you are practicing (or are being practiced on you). Now you have to decide to change and figure out how you are going to change. Then you have to change. Don't think you can do it all at once or that it will happen overnight. It took a long time to develop your bad habits, so it will take a long time to change them. But it is never too late to start.

I will not try to give you details on what to do about each time waster, but here are some hints. Many of them will be treated in more detail later in this book.

- Learn how and when to say no and when to refer a problem to someone else.
- Make sure you know what your priorities are, and make sure what you are doing contributes to accomplishing them.
- Plan for the unexpected. Allow time for emergencies, interruptions, and uninvited visitors.
- Stop complaining, feeling sorry for yourself, being angry, or feeling guilty. It will get you nowhere. If you can do something about a problem, do it; if not, let it go.
- Never promise what you cannot deliver. When in doubt, don't.
- Attend only those meetings that need *your* presence and that will help you advance your goals.
- Do not be a perfectionist. Let others do what you cannot or should not do. Delegating allows you to be more efficient and your colleagues to learn. (See the quiz in the box at the end of this list.)
- Do not micromanage or let anyone micromanage you. The best management is the least management.
- Do not let people interrupt you, and do not interrupt others.
- Use waiting time for something productive.
- Leave complete telephone messages for other people to avoid telephone tag.
- Always backup anything of importance that you entrust to a computer.

- Realize that technology, computers, and other office machines are here to make our lives easier, not for us to become their slaves. If it is easier, faster, better, or cheaper to do it manually, then do it manually.
- Make sure all rules and procedures in your library make sense. Make sure there *are* procedures for any repetitive tasks, and make sure they are followed.
- Read efficiently and only what you need to read.
- Bundle like tasks, such as errands, copying, and asking questions of your boss. Do errands at off-hours to minimize waiting.
- Shop by mail or from vendors that deliver.
- Organize your workspace—your desk, your files, your computer. Make sure you can find what you need.
- Do not procrastinate. If you are not sure where to start, just start somewhere.
- Do not make snap decisions (without sufficient information), but do make a decision.
- Never handle a piece of paper (or e-mail) without doing something to help move it along—and off your desk.
- Have a plan. Know where you are going and how you intend to get there. Keep your goals in mind at all times.
- Make the first two hours of your day the most productive by doing only high-priority tasks.
- Make sure that a rush is really a rush and an emergency is really an emergency—and one in which you need to be involved. Do not take on other people's problems.
- Listen and communicate effectively. Do not write unless you have to. Make sure you understand all directions given to you, and make sure you give clear instructions to others.
- Use the Internet for communication and reference, but be aware that it can also be a giant time sink.

Pedley (4) says:

One of the biggest time wasters ever invented is the Internet. When you search the Internet you can easily lose track of time, and after spending three quarters of an hour searching for an obscure topic you might still come away without an answer to a difficult enquiry. If you were charging by the hour, you would be keeping a very close watch on how much time you had spent on a particular task, so don't be afraid to impose a limit on how long you spend on a specific enquiry. Sometimes it is more cost effective to pay for a market research report, for example, than it is to try and find the answer on the web for free.

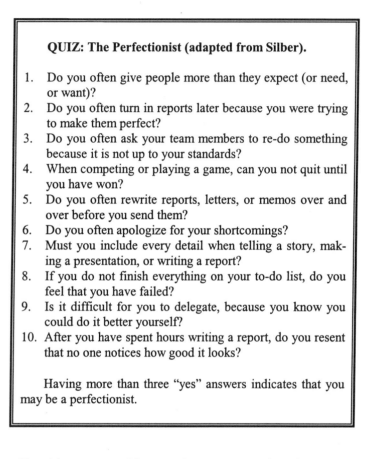

QUIZ: The Perfectionist (adapted from Silber).

1. Do you often give people more than they expect (or need, or want)?
2. Do you often turn in reports later because you were trying to make them perfect?
3. Do you often ask your team members to re-do something because it is not up to your standards?
4. When competing or playing a game, can you not quit until you have won?
5. Do you often rewrite reports, letters, or memos over and over before you send them?
6. Do you often apologize for your shortcomings?
7. Must you include every detail when telling a story, making a presentation, or writing a report?
8. If you do not finish everything on your to-do list, do you feel that you have failed?
9. Is it difficult for you to delegate, because you know you could do it better yourself?
10. After you have spent hours writing a report, do you resent that no one notices how good it looks?

Having more than three "yes" answers indicates that you may be a perfectionist.

Now it's your turn. List your time wasters, and work on one at a time—for a couple of weeks or until you eliminate it (or determine that it cannot be eliminated—no need to get compulsive about this). Then pick another and repeat, being careful not to relapse on the one or ones already eliminated. See Appendix B for some forms you can use for this.

Make the Best Use of Time

Just as everything you do is not of equal importance or value, every time of the day is not equal. Some people work best in the morning, some in the afternoon. Some tasks require your full concentration, some only need a part of your attention. The tricks are knowing when to work and what to do when.

There are many ways to classify time. One is by length:

- **Fragments (short periods).** Have a list of 10-minute jobs, such as reading mail, drafting letters, leaving phone messages, or day-dreaming—a vastly under-rated activity. Find things that can be done in the "in-between," small pieces of time (5 to 10 minutes). Return calls, sign letters, clean your desk, go over your to-do list, go through your mail, write a note, relax, or read items in your "to-read" file.

- **Big blocks (at least an hour of uninterrupted time).** Use this only for high-priority projects or tasks requiring concentration. Large blocks of time are very rare for librarians and should not be wasted on routine or low-priority activities. You may need to escape the library to use this time. Find a place that you can "hide" and not be found. (I used the company mailroom. Since I was usually hiding from my boss, it was perfect. I doubt if he even knew there was a mailroom.)

- **Found time.** Also called "free" time or time windfalls, found time is "unexpected periods of idle time" (Cochran, 31). For example, your meeting or appointment was canceled. Make good use of the time by reading professional journals, making telephone calls, writing memos, and so on. You can also use found time for those little jobs that you just have not been able to get around to doing (www.123sortit.com, Self Management).

- **Invisible or created time.** You make this time by being early to meetings or appointments. Use it in the same way as found time.

2

Learning to Use Time More Efficiently and More Effectively

The Librarian's Dilemma

What are my problems? "Too much stuff to do, too little time."

An independent information broker

Librarians face special time challenges because of the very nature of our jobs and our personalities. We became librarians because we like helping people. Libraries are oriented to provide service to their users. Many librarians feel that the principles of time management—planning, prioritization, and saying no—are not compatible with good library practice. Rather than conflicting with the traditions of librarianship, time management is the key to reaching our service goals. "Employing good time management techniques enables librarians to accomplish more, thus allowing them to serve more of the library's clientele while also bringing them closer to realizing their own professional and personal goals" (Cochran, 6).

Most of our clients are drop-ins. Very few people call ahead to set up a search or make a reservation to check out a book. We feel we must be available to everyone, all the time. We do not prioritize or plan, and we meekly accept interruptions. "At the end of the work day, too often it seems that librarians have little to show for their efforts" (Cochran, 5). There are still items to be cataloged, reference questions to be answered, books to be shelved, and periodicals to be checked in—and often as many at the end of the day as at the beginning.

The ultimate time-challenged libraries are those staffed by only one person—the kind I have worked in most of my career. Walster says,

> Librarians in one-person libraries are subjected to the maximum time challenge from the two roles of service provider and manager. They must be all things to all people. In addition, they serve as their own clerical staff. Setting priorities is essential . . . in order to function in all capacities successfully. Using time management techniques and principles can help the librarian in the one-person library [and in larger libraries as well] streamline routine, clerical, and managerial tasks. Time management cannot help librarians complete all possible tasks. They cannot all be done, no matter how efficient, effective, and responsible librarians are in their time management. This limitation must be accepted.

Why don't more librarians practice good time management? "Too many librarians . . . do not manage their time well because they have never been taught how to do so. Few professional schools introduce their graduates to time management" (Cochran, 4). Little of the professional literature teaches or even deals with time management, planning (other than for large or public libraries), or—especially—prioritization. In addition, library continuing education is seldom available in these areas. When someone is sent for training, usually it is not the library manager. The manager is the one who sets the tone for the organization. The poor time management skills of managers make the lives of their subordinates much harder. "Time management needs to go from top to bottom, not bottom to top. It's a waste of money for a company to send people at lower and middle management when the people above have poor [time management] skills" (Kenneth Zeigler in Abernathy, 24). So, after you have read this book, do not keep your newly improved time management techniques secret. Teach them to your staff, your colleagues, even your boss.

Why Manage Your Time

Planning your day, rather than allowing it to unfold at the whim of others, is the single most important piece in the time management puzzle.

Alec Mackenzie

The advantages of managing your time better are that you 1) get more done, 2) reduce your stress, and 3) have more time to do what you want to do (Nauman, 40). But first you have to accept the fact that, for the most part, you are to blame for your own problems. Time itself is not what needs to be controlled. It is our attitude toward time and our use of it that need to change. "Becoming more conscious of the choices you make and learning to reclaim some of these choices is the very essence of effective time management" (Marshall J. Cook, 60). As Golda Meir said, "I must govern the clock, not be governed by it"(in McGee-Cooper, 3).

EXERCISE: Are you in control of your time? (adapted from Winston).

(Answer always, most of the time, sometimes, rarely, or never.)

1. I know what my most urgent tasks are for today.
2. I get them done.
3. I do not miss deadlines.
4. I know how my staff is doing on their projects.
5. I match my tasks to my own energy cycle.
6. I delegate tasks that others can do.
7. I am interrupted no more than three times a day.
8. I do not procrastinate.
9. I return telephone calls promptly.
10. My daily tasks match my long-term goals.

What It Takes

Knowing what to do is not the same as doing it. Doing takes commitment, time, patience, and knowledge. "Knowledge is the . . . *what to do* and the *why*. Skill is the *how to do*. And desire is the motivation, the *want to do*. In order to make something a habit in our lives, we have to have all three" (Covey, 12–13). "In order to change a behavioral pattern, however, it is necessary to understand the reasons for that behavior" (Berner, 24).

By now, you know that you waste time and why. What's next? Time management need not be complicated or difficult, "but librarians are challenged so often that they tend to become accustomed to expecting the difficult. As a result, sometimes they may overlook the obvious" (Cochran, 16). It really is easier than you think.

You need to commit yourself to change. One good way to do this is by telling others what you are doing, including how you will make the change. This gives you that much more incentive to be successful; you do not want to fail in front of others. Begin soon—today is best. You do not need to change everything at once. Start with one behavior or just try to improve by 10 percent. Incremental change, the law of the slight edge, applies here. "Small changes over time make big differences" (Clark and Clark, 17). Practice the new technique every day for at least three weeks. Once it is perfected, attack another habit, then another, and another. Soon you will have exchanged your bad time management habits for new, more effective ones. You will not necessarily succeed the first time you try to change. Accept the setback, and continue your new behavior. Discipline is learned; it is not something you are born with.

A habit is not the same as a routine. "A habit is a *behavior* you conduct regularly and without thought. A routine is a customary *procedure* for doing something" (Allen, 28). A routine is the result of forethought—thinking out the right way to do something. Routines reduce wasted time, errors, tension, and the learning curve; routines increase productivity and your success rate.

Also remember that the time management process is never done. Your time management problems will change over time, with changes in jobs, co-workers, interests, and so on. Old problems may reappear. Be aware, and be flexible. You may have to apply the process over and over again, seemingly starting over.

Efficiency versus Effectiveness

A key way to use your time well is to be both efficient and effective. Efficiency is completing a task with the least possible amount of wasted labor, money, or time. Effectiveness refers to the quality of the work. Efficiency means finding the best way to do a particular job, whatever the job might be. Effectiveness means examining a range of tasks, selecting the most important to be completed, and then completing them. "Being effective is choosing the right goals from a set of alternatives and reaching them. Efficiency, on the other hand, assumes the goals as given and proper and proceeds to find the best means of achieving them. . . . Effectiveness means results . . . [and] is far more important" (LeBoeuf, 9). An efficient person does things well, focuses on activities, and is busy. An effective person does things that matter, focuses on results, and is productive (Weeks, 6). In short, efficiency means doing things right, whereas effectiveness means doing the right things.

You can become more efficient by eliminating useless, time-consuming activities; making sure the effort matches the objective; standardizing, using forms; consolidating or grouping like tasks; outsourcing or delegating; rearranging your workspace; and, most importantly, planning or anticipating the future. Do not confuse "busyness" with efficiency. The best people in an organization sometimes spend their most productive time seemingly daydreaming. Busyness may, in fact, be counterproductive. James D. Watson, co-discoverer of the genetic code of DNA, once said, "It is necessary to be slightly underemployed if you are to do something significant" (in Griessman, 47).

Effectiveness is a bit more complicated. "Look around your company and see how many activities are at least one level from something that improves the effectiveness of the people or the quality of the product" (Adams, 316). Repeated corporate restructuring or unceasing budget activity are anti-effectiveness. Make sure you are doing the right things. "Eighty percent of your boss's satisfaction with you is related to only 20 percent of the work you perform. Your first task in learning to be as effective as possible is to find out what that 20 percent is. Then be certain that you put your attention on that 20 percent (St. James, 142).

Finally, doing the right things well is the epitome of efficiency *and* effectiveness. This is the Holy Grail of time management.

Getting Organized

Organization is a close cousin to time management.

Jan Jasper

In *Organizing from the Inside Out* (Turner), Morgenstern says:

Organizing is the process [by] which we create environments that enable [us] to live, work, and relax exactly as we want to. When we are organized, our homes, offices, and schedules reflect and encourage who we are, what we want, and where are going It's not natural to stop and reflect when disorganization is at its peak. The impulse is to just dive in and attack. But if you invest a little time doing some thinking and analysis first, you will be able to zero in on just the right solution for you.

According to the American Demographics Society, "Americans waste nine million hours a day looking for misplaced items. *The Wall Street Journal* reported that the average U.S. executive wastes six weeks per year (an hour a day) searching for missing information in messy desks and files" (Morgenstern in Turner). In addition, in 1999 an American television reporter said that each day the average office worker receives 30 e-mails, 22 voice mails, 18 pieces of postal mail, 15 faxes, and 11 Post-it notes™ (Potter).

Organization is not the same as neatness. It is not restricting; rather, it is liberating: "It will free you to be more creative and more spontaneous, with time to do things you never before had time for" (Jasper, 10). "Being organized is not an end in itself—it is a vehicle to take you from where you are to where you want to be" (Winston, 25). If this is what organization is not, what *is* organization? In the *10 Minute Guide to Managing Your Time*, Davidson (50) defines being organized as "arranging one's possessions, time, or life so as to remain comfortably in control." That's the key—being comfortably in control. It need not be difficult or complicated.

Organization is also highly individualistic. To one person a neat desk is easier to work on; to another it is intimidating. One person's filing system is often incomprehensible to another person. "A good system expresses the organization of your mind in the environment. It is designed to place in your hands the tools and techniques that will enable you to achieve your goals through skillful management of time, paper, and people" (Winston, 25). Organize yourself in a way that fits the way you work. And do not spend a lot of time doing it. Over-organization is as bad as under-organization. Both waste time that could be better used in another manner.

Organizing Audit (adapted from Winston).

1. Does it often take you longer than one minute to find something on your desk?
2. Does it often take you longer than five minutes to find something in your files?
3. Have you ever had to improvise because you were missing an important piece of information?

4. Do you often file things just in case you might need them again?

5. Would it take more than 30 minutes to file everything in your to-file box?

6. Do you often find duplicate items in your files (that you did not put there deliberately)?

7. Do you have an index to your files?

8. Do you sometimes go more than a day without meeting with your assistant?

9. Do you only hold staff meetings when a crisis occurs?

10. Does your staff frequently misunderstand your instructions?

11. Have you ever been surprised to find that one of your projects is behind schedule?

12. Do you regularly find items in your "to-read" folder of items that are months old?

13. Do you regularly take work home?

14. Have you ever lost an important memo or letter that you were supposed to answer right away?

15. Does your boss often have to call *you* to follow up on a project?

16. Have you recently forgotten an appointment, date, or meeting?

17. Do you frequently put off starting a project until it becomes an emergency?

18. Has anyone ever complained that your reports are too long and rambling?

19. Are you way behind on reading your professional journals?

20. Are you so caught up in your everyday routine that you do not have time for long-range planning?

The more "yes" answers you have, the more you need to get organized.

We can find lots of excuses for not being organized. 1) "There is not enough time; if I take time to organize it will take time away from higher-priority tasks." As long as you do not overorganize, a few minutes now will save more time later when you don't have to hunt all over for what you need. 2) "I don't have time to do it right; and if I can't do it right, then I won't do it at all." This is just an excuse to avoid organizing. Who is to define what is the "right" way to organize. Anyway, some organization is better than no organization. Chaos is not creativity. 3) "I don't know how." That's why I wrote this book. Read on.

The real problem with organizing is human. "Whatever ultra-sophisticated tools one may possess organization is ultimately up to the person using them" (Allen, 1). Being disorganized does not make you a bad person; it only makes you a disorganized person. "Organization is a learned skill you just haven't gotten around to yet. Organizing is active and personal. It's a process, and it's about you" (Turner). Turner continues:

> Organizing is a skill, like learning to tie your shoes, rather than an innate talent. Organizing can create great excitement by clearing away physical and mental clutter. Organizing is worth the time it takes away from other tasks. In fact, you should build time into each day for organizing and maintaining that organization. Without this modern survival skill, you will likely spend your time on urgent but unimportant items.

Organization is learned, not inborn. To start, "Think of one thing in your life that is disorganized and that would not take a lot of time and effort to straighten out. Designate a specific time in the next three days to take care of it" (Tullier, 4). At a minimum, you will want to have a place for everything and keep it there, deal with important stuff immediately, make to-do lists (and act on them), and have a daily routine (Tullier, 106). To this I would add that you should create a personal and professional strategic plan with goals and priorities, and an action plan for achieving them.

Winston (28–29) suggests the following methodology for getting organized:

1. List your primary job tasks.
2. List the major challenges to your organization or library (e.g., downsizing, finances, and so on).
3. Decide which of your primary job tasks relate most closely to the major challenges.
4. List the most common impediments to accomplishing your primary job tasks that you regularly encounter.
5. Make a regular appointment with yourself for organizing (e.g., an hour a week or 15 minutes a day).
6. Tackle the worst of the impediments in the first session—which should be as soon as possible.
7. Work down your list, one problem per session.
8. Review steps 1 to 3, making changes as needed.

9. Regularly (perhaps monthly), review your solutions to make sure that you do not backslide.

"Don't expect any product [including this book] to organize you. You have to do the work" (Pollar, 106). But there are many tools to assist you. Several companies make organizer software (*see* Appendix A). You can use low-tech solutions to organize yourself and your workspace: Post-it notes; Rolodex® cards (use the 4-by-6 size, because you can clip business cards to it and still have room to make notes); 3-by-5 index cards; daily, weekly, or monthly planners; and even the humble desk calendar (either the two-page-per-day or blotter size will work). If you do not find a commercial product that fits your personal style, you can always create your own.

Timing

Knowing when not to work is as important as knowing when to.

Harvey McKay

Timing is important in knowing when to work and when not to. Look at your workday routine. Is it efficient? Does it fit your personal clock? If not, change it.

The temporary employment firm Accountemps found that 51 percent of their customers say that Tuesday is the most productive day of the week (Abernathy, 24). For most people the first two hours of the day are the most productive. Avoid scheduling meetings for this time. Do not eat breakfast at work, exclude others (except for brief greetings), do not look at your in-box or e-mail, and arrange to be uninterrupted. Do the things you do not want to do first—you will avoid the stress of anticipating doing them. Take a bit of time first thing to look at your daily plan, and get a good idea of what you need to get done that day.

I think it is better to look at the next day at the end of the previous day. Doing so lets you look back and see what you have accomplished and give yourself credit for it, gets you ready for a personal life, and gives you a jump start on the next day. "Stop constructively . . . on a high note. If you quit at a point of satisfaction, you will tend to think of the work as gratifying and be more eager to return to it. If you quit at a point where you're stalled, write down the problem. . . . Have a logical starting point at which to resume" (Le Boeuf, 54).

At the end of the day, check e-mail, check voice mail, go through the mail and "to-do" files, review what you want to do the next day. You will feel better when you leave and can leave the office at the office. Silber (88) says to save the "easiest tasks for the end of the day." You accomplish something and go home satisfied, not frustrated.

A routine helps you get started in the morning because you know what you should be doing. I really like the idea of doing the hard tasks at the beginning of the day when you are fresh, and saving the easy tasks for the end of the day when you need to wind things up and go home feeling good. No matter what time of day, it is important to stay focused on high-priority activities and limit the time you spend on low-priority tasks, no matter how easy or how much fun they are.

Time-Use Analysis

The most important tool for time management is a time audit or time log. A time audit is similar to a financial audit. First, you need to find out how much time you have—30, 40, or 48 hours, or whatever number of hours you are expected or willing to work. Then you need to see how your time is spent—the time log. Only then can you decide how to manage your time.

Step One. Estimate how you think you use your time. Write down the tasks that are part of your job and the amount of time (in hours or percentages) you think you spend on each. "Much of a librarian's workday consists of recurring tasks, work normally done every day, such as cataloging books or answering reference questions. In establishing the daily work and appointment schedule, a librarian should know about how much of the day should be devoted to these recurring tasks" (Cochran, 25).

Step Two. See how you actually use your time. Keep a time log. Make up a sheet or grid with all the tasks in Step One. (Examples of time logs are given in Appendix B.) You will need one log for every day of the study and one for a summary. You will also need space to add those activities you did not anticipate.

You should keep your log for at least a week. Doing it for two weeks or more will yield better, more representative data, however. This will minimize the effect of an out-of-ordinary day or a big project. You may even want to do the process again at another time of the year.

Record everything that you do. Include the time you spend at the water cooler or coffee or tea bar, chatting with a colleague, talking on the phone, looking in your files, dealing with short interruptions, opening the mail, and even daydreaming. It is essential that you make a record as you go, not after the fact. When you make a telephone call, write down the name of the person you call, the general topic, and how long you talk. One technique I like is "Every single time you shift your attention, record the new item. Don't make the common mistake of noting what you're doing at fixed intervals, say every fifteen minutes; you simply miss too much that way" (Mackenzie, 46). Law librarians may have an advantage here if they are already logging their time for billing purposes.

At the end of the log period, summarize each day and the entire day. Include the actual time and percentage of time spent on each category and your pre-log category estimates. Do not do the summaries every day, because the results may influence how you use your time the next day.

Step Three. Determine how you want to use your time. Compare your estimated and actual usage of time. Where do they differ? Why? Where are you wasting time? How much of your time is spent on routine tasks that could be delegated or outsourced? How much of your time is being spent on high-priority tasks? Now that you can see how you really use your time, I can almost guarantee that there will be some surprises.

Step Four. Make the necessary changes. You will not be able to make them overnight, but keep working on it. Make daily schedules and planning guides, calendars, to-do lists, and weekly plans; and improve your time management techniques. (Appendix B has sample forms that you can copy or adapt.)

Step Five. Repeat Steps Two through Four periodically to make sure you remain on track. "At least every few months, choose one day [or more; see above] and keep [a] careful log of how you actually spend your time during that day" (Stanley Smith, 17). You are bound to backslide in some areas occasionally. Do not panic, just go back to your plan.

Here is a potpourri of time management hints.

- Carry pen or pencil and a pad of paper (or Post-it notes) with you at all times.
- Write down thoughts (or questions) as they occur to you.
- Use multitasking to get more done.
- Always have something to read or do while you wait.
- Simplify. Examine every repetitive task you perform to see if you can streamline it.
- "Set aside a certain day to work on various library routines to prevent things from piling up" (Cochran, 35).

- If it costs more to do it yourself than to hire someone to do it, hire someone.
- Use document delivery or fax rather than physically going and getting it.
- Pace yourself.
- Get in the habit of being ahead of time—it is less stressful.
- *Time shift*, that is, do things at other than normal working hours to avoid wasting time waiting in line; shop or do errands during the week, not at lunch, on Saturday, or evenings.
- Leave 20% of your time unscheduled to deal with interruptions (Corcoran, 111).
- Divide large or difficult tasks into smaller, easier parts.
- Set a time to be undisturbed.
- Find a place to hide.
- Do not overschedule; be flexible.
- Deal with emergencies by preventing them when you can.
- "Don't accept a task until you understand the 'why' of it, not just the 'what' of it" (Pollar, 80).
- "Going the cheap route is often more expensive" (Pollar, 71). Do it right, not cheap.
- Make a checklist for things you do regularly, such as organizing meetings, presentations, new book processing, or packing for a trip. Keep your checklists so that you don't have to redo them.
- Use a timer or alarm clock to tell you when it is time to make an important telephone call, get up and stretch or walk around, or leave for an appointment; or use it to signal when half the time you have allotted to a project (or visitor, or call) is up so you can concentrate on the project (St. James, 92–93).
- Give yourself an extra day after vacation to catch up. Tell people you will not be in until the 6th, but return the 5th and catch up (St. James, 41). I often came in over the weekend or at night, when I would not be undisturbed. (Just make sure that it is *your* decision.) As an OPL, I found it took a minimum of three days to catch up after being gone for a week; allow for about one day of catch-up for one day out.

Procrastination

You miss 100 percent of the shots you never take.

Wayne Gretzky, hockey great (in Silber, 101)

The last of Berner's Three Ps is (Siess)

. . . not something that you should work towards, but something that you should avoid, and that is procrastination. Accept the fact that everyone procrastinates sometimes, and understand that guilt will not help to solve the problem. It is very important, however, to keep in mind that you should not assume that because everyone procrastinates it cannot be a serious problem. It can, in fact, rob you of your effectiveness on the job. No matter what you may think and no matter what you may have convinced yourself over the years, no one works best under pressure. Procrastination only insures that you will have to rush to complete a project, and that you will have insufficient time to check your work and to create a superior product. Procrastination leaves no time for that great despoiler of work: Murphy's Law. If you leave yourself ample time for a project and something goes wrong, you'll be able to correct it and still meet your deadline. Without that sufficient time, however, your work will suffer, and no doubt your reputation will suffer along with it.

The Procrastinator's Creed

I believe that if anything were worth doing, it would have been done already.

I shall meet all of my deadlines directly in proportion to the amount of bodily injury I could expect to receive from missing them.

I firmly believe that tomorrow holds the possibility for new technologies, astounding discoveries, and a reprieve from my obligations.

I truly believe that all deadlines are unreasonable regardless of the amount of time given.

I shall never forget that the probability of a miracle, though infinitesimally small, is not exactly zero.

If at first I don't succeed, there is always next year.

I shall always decide not to decide, unless of course I decide to change my mind.

I obey the law of inverse excuses which demands that the greater the task to be done, the more insignificant the work that must be done prior to beginning the greater task.

I know that the work cycle is not plan/start/finish, but is wait/plan/plan.

I will never put off until tomorrow what I can forget about forever.

From Deb's Fun Pages, www.debsfunpages.com/creed.htm, 25 March 2001; with permission.

Why We Procrastinate

There are many reasons for procrastination. When the task seems so daunting or large that you do not know where to start, divide the task into smaller parts and start somewhere. Anywhere will do, as long as you start. If it is something that you do not want to do, you might as well get it over with. You cannot avoid it forever. Some experts advise doing unpleasant tasks first thing in the day so that you do not have time to dread them. If you are afraid of failing, realize that failure is not a bad thing, assuming you learn from your mistakes. I have never heard of an organization going under because of a librarian's mistake, nor are many librarians fired because of one error. If you do not have the information you need to do a task, get the information and get on with it. Librarians are the information experts; we know how to find information. If you think that if you put it off, someone else will do the task (called *negative delegation*), know that this seldom works. One prioritization technique involves ignoring a task to see if anyone misses it, but that is a different matter.

Other common excuses for procrastination (note that I used the term *excuses* instead of *reasons*, because procrastination is never acceptable) are an over-commitment to other projects (you haven't said "no" enough) or lack of motivation because you believe the task will not make a difference anyway. (If you think that, you have other problems.) "Many people procrastinate because they're lonely. It feels isolating to tackle a task alone with no one there to cheer you on. Tell [a] person what you need to accomplish by what date, and ask him to check in on your progress" (Goulston and Goldberg in Beam, 4). "Think of someone, a teacher perhaps, who has believed in you in the past and would want you to [do] the right thing now. Have a conversation in your mind, and let this person coach you and inspire you to tackle your project" (Beam).

What else can you do to overcome procrastination? List the things you have been avoiding. Prioritize them. Try to do at least one of them each day until you catch up. SWAP, that is, Start With A Part, break it down into smaller parts, and tackle just one part. Remember that it is not procrastination if you put aside a low-priority project to work on a high-priority one. Also remember that you do not work best under pressure. No one does. This is just a rationalization for procrastination.

What Is Procrastination?

Tullier (18) defines *procrastination* as "the act of putting off something until later by either not starting it, starting it at the last minute, or starting but not finishing." The word comes from the Latin words *pro*, which means for, and *cras*, which means tomorrow. "You don't procrastinate because you're a bad person or because you're a bad librarian. [However,] procrastination isn't harmless, and it isn't something that affects only you" (Berner, 26). One of the dangers of procrastination is that it is contagious.

There are many kinds of procrastination. Stanley Smith (33) divides them into conscious, when we are aware of what we are doing, and unconscious. Similar to conscious procrastination is Porat's (1) "creative procrastination," the "planned and deliberate gift of prime time to yourself each day to do what gives you greatest satisfaction, including not doing anything, if that is your choice." Porat (xiii) also describes "negative procrastination—those idle and unplanned uses of time which block us from achieving a more fulfilled life," which seems similar to Smith's unconscious procrastination.

Bruno (2–4) describes five kinds of procrastination:

1. *Functional:* done for a good reason, such as insufficient information, illness, or because a higher-priority task came up.
2. *Dysfunctional:* useless or self-defeating behavior.
3. *Short-term:* when you are just a few hours or days late.
4. *Long-term:* when you never get around to something.
5. *Chronic:* a combination of dysfunctional and long-term.

Interruptions can be a form of passive procrastination. If you let people interrupt you, you can avoid working on what you do not want to do. Not saying "no" is another form of procrastination because if you *have* to do everything your customers ask, you can avoid doing the important—but hard—tasks. Insisting on researching a subject beyond a certain point is also a form of procrastination. Do not succumb to over-analysis, over-organization, and underaction. In a similar vein, you can spend too much time making a report look perfect. The content of reports is more important that the format. You do not have to be perfect, just good. Frequently, good enough is good enough. As for doing things at the last minute or waiting for that adrenaline rush, Tullier suggests that by putting things off until the last minute and then heroically getting it done, you make yourself look good—to yourself and others. Think about how this delay affects those around you.

Procrastination can also look like real work. Cartoonist and humorist Scott Adams describes "Dilbert's Total Work Equation: Real Work + Appearance of Work = Total Work" (Adams, 93). He gives these examples of the appearance of work: Internet surfing, writing and reading personal e-mail, attending meetings, talking to your boss, attending conventions (not for librarians—we *need* to attend professional conferences), waiting for answers from co-workers, and hiding behind voice mail. To this I would add reading, doing everything yourself, running away, or excessive socializing.

Overcoming Procrastination

Start! The only way to finish a project is to start!

A librarian at an information research firm

"Procrastination is not, of course, something that happens to you. It is not forced upon you by external circumstances. Instead, it is something that you *do*" (Bruno, vii). Therefore, you *can* stop doing it. Here are some hints to get *you* started.

Recognize the futility of putting things off. You don't want to do anything right now? Try doing absolutely nothing. You'll find it hard. List the things you have been avoiding. Prioritize them. Try to do at least one of them each day until you catch up. Put off only low-priority tasks.

Change how you think. Listen to your thoughts, feelings, and words. Think positively. Don't say, "I can't," or "I don't." Don't predict failure that may not happen. Yes, if you make a mistake you could lose your job. But it is unlikely that one mistake will get you fired and besides, "many librarians have sought and found jobs on short notice, so the real effect of a bad decision is likely to be minimal" (Cochran, 31).

Do not be too critical of yourself. Think about what could go wrong, and prepare for it. Try some of Bruno's Mind Tricks (42–45): Imagine the "reason" for your procrastination as a "tissue-paper barrier," not a stone wall, and break through; "apply the seat of the pants to the seat of the chair" and start—anywhere; "don't tell yourself a task is difficult, tell yourself it is challenging." Put some fun into the task.

If you are having trouble starting a project, focus on starting, not finishing. But if starting is important, finishing is critical. Think how good you will feel when the job is done. Define the problem, establish priorities, start with the most important item, get the information you need, list subtasks, and reward yourself for starting. "Nothing is particularly hard if you divide it into small jobs" (Henry Ford in Bly, 21).

"Most tasks do not go away, they just get added to" (Nauman, 22). "Hard work is often the easy work you did not do at the proper time" (Bernard Meltzer in Abernathy, 24). That unpleasant small task is now an unpleasant big one, so do not aggravate yourself about it, just do it.

Get the boring tasks out of the way as fast as possible. If you really cannot stand doing something, do it only for, say, 30 minutes at a time, then take a break and reward yourself. Rewards for *not* procrastinating are better than punishments for procrastination. Stick with a task until it is done. "Some of the work in the operation of a library is not particularly interesting or stimulating, but it has to be done for the library to run smoothly." Postponing these "boring" tasks can "impair the library's mission of prompt delivery of information services" (Cochran, 32).

Some tasks "require speed more than perfection." Do them quick and dirty (McGee-Cooper, 109). "Anything that'll take two minutes, do it right then" (Jasper, 82). But beware! If you keep doing the quick tasks, you might not get around to the important ones. Take advantage of your moods. If you are not in the mood to do one thing, do another you *are* in the mood to do. Every day, do at least *some* work on your goal.

Assign consequences to missed deadlines. Think like this: Late = Penalty (Allen, 56). Then stick to the deadline. To avoid missed deadlines, start earlier and allow more time. Build in flexibility so that interruptions will not throw you off. You *do not* work best under pressure—no one does. This is just rationalization.

Deal with problems when they occur. When you postpone dealing with a problem, you waste time dreading it. But you *still* have to deal with it. The delay probably will make the problem worse, and then it will take longer to deal with. "Delay is rarely beneficial. Recognize the greater unpleasantness, work, money, time and stress that result from postponing a decision [or task]" (Pollar, 65).

When at a dead end on a project, leave it for a while. More work on it now will just be a waste of time. Come back to it later with fresh eyes.

Dealing with Data

The 80/20 rule, a derivative of Pareto's Principle, applies to your office—whether you're a household manager or corporate executive. We use about 20 percent of what we have. The other 80 percent is no longer of value to us. Your aim is to sort 100 percent of your office, purge the unused 80 percent, and organize the useful 20 percent.

Anne Marie Turner

The following are paper-management myths and truths:

1. *Myth:* Piles are bad. *Truth:* Not if you can find things.
2. *Myth:* A messy desk is a sign of a messy mind. *Truth:* Some people are not comfortable with a clean desk.
3. *Myth:* An empty in-box is the goal. *Truth:* You don't need to do everything immediately. "Don't be the slave of your in-box. Just because something's there doesn't mean you have to do it" (Malcolm S. Forbes, Jr., in Griessman, 86).
4. *Myth:* Handle paper only once. *Truth:* This is an impossible and unnecessary rule. "The myth of handling each piece of paper once must give way to the reality that most pieces of paper should never cross your desk at all (Davidson, *10 Minute Guide. . .* , 6). "Although the adage 'handle a piece of paper only once' sounds great in theory, it's not practical unless you can complete everything that comes your way by the end of the day. You can at least resolve to move everything out of your in-box after handling it once" (Hemphill and Gibbard, 72).
5. *Myth:* A clean, sterile environment is best for the workplace. *Truth:* Only for doctors and dentists.
6. *Myth:* If you haven't used it in a year, toss it. *Truth:* No, just be selective.
7. *Myth:* File everything. *Truth:* Again, be selective.

Remember all the predictions of the paperless society? Forget them. We now deal with more paper than ever—in addition to all that electronic data. Where does all this data come from? LeBoeuf (143–145) suggests four reasons:

- *Government regulations and output.* The computer makes it so much easier for the government—and most other organizations—to generate data.
- *The information explosion.* More information is generated every day than we could ever consume.
- *Copier, (fax machines, and printers).* Although very useful, these machines have made it too easy to generate paper.

- *A lack of trust.* We do not trust each other, so we ask for things in writing. We do not trust the computer, so we save it on paper—just in case.

Winston (38) has a different idea. "The real cause of a paperwork crisis is a problem with decision-making, picking up the same piece of paper five times and putting it down again because you can't decide what to do with it." We have to be willing to make sure that when we handle a piece of paper or data we do *something* to move it along its way out of our workspace. Of course, this is not as easy as it seems.

Your in-boxes: The first place to start is your in-boxes—the physical one on your desk and the virtual one in your e-mail program. If the item is a low-priority one, do something with it immediately. Do not let it clutter your desk or mind. "Sort through your in-box [only] two or three times a day" (Stanley Smith, 31). Resist the temptation to react to every addition as soon as it comes in. This is especially true of e-mail. If there is something you cannot deal with right away, put it in either your "Hold" file or the appropriate action folder ("To-read," "To-pay," and so on). At the same time, put a note on your calendar for when you need to deal with it (Winston, 40). That way you will not forget about it. (Out of sight, out of mind is not a good management technique.) Some of your incoming paper contains information that simply needs to be recorded for future use: calendar entries for meetings and social gatherings; contact information for your rotary file, planner notebook, or technology-based contact manager; and reminders for your to-do list (Turner). If you find your overflowing in-box to be depressing, think about whether you are attempting too much. Maybe you need to be more selective about the tasks you accept.

Managing Your To-Read Pile

I have never talked to a librarian who felt that he or she was able to keep up with professional reading. Accept the fact that you will probably never be able to read everything you would like to (or think you ought to). It is not your fault that you cannot keep up. No one can. "More words are published or broadcast *in an hour* than you could comfortably ingest in the rest of your life" (Davidson, *The Complete Idiot's Guide to Managing Your Time*, 29).

"Effective reading involves knowing what to read as well as how to read it. Just because there's information available to you doesn't mean that you need it" (Pollar, 8). Because you never know when some fact will come in handy, however, learn to triage your reading. Skim everything and decide whether it is important or interesting and must be read, whether you should read it only if you have time, or whether it is not important and can be thrown away. Read with a pen in your hand.

Concentrate on just the most important journals in your field. "I don't have to read and learn everything that comes in. It is enough to skim the journals and get an idea of what is in them. I'm a librarian; if I need articles on Information Auditing someday, I should be able to find them" (an independent information broker). A quick scan is better than a complete reading that is never done. Peruse the table of contents. Rip out articles you want to read. Put them in a folder you can take with you. If you do not want to tear out articles, at least mark them with a Post-it note on the front of the magazine. You can tear out the articles of interest and file them for further reference without reading them, but then you run the risk of them being outdated by the time you need them. A better way is to set up a current awareness search for library journals just for yourself and your staff (Todaro, 134); use a table of contents service, such as *The Informed Librarian*; or, better yet, split the reading with your staff or a colleague. Before you renew a subscription, stop and ask yourself: "Do I really *need* this? "If I haven't read/browsed a magazine within 30 days of receipt, I toss it. And then I think about whether I need to renew that subscription next year" (a paralegal and information specialist).

For most things, you should read only the summaries or just the introduction and conclusions. Periodically, ask yourself if you *really* need to see all the reports you get? If not, try to get off the lists. Do the same with routing lists. But don't be too ruthless; as a librarian you need to know what is going on. However, there are some things you should read completely: interoffice "memos, particularly from Finance or Administration, to avoid being blindsided by a change in policy that can adversely affect the library down the road. Keep current with internal changes" (Tomlin, 8). This also goes for organizational business plans.

When your "To-read" folder gets too full, "take the back handful and toss it without looking at it because it's the oldest" (Jane Yoos in Tolpa). If you have not read it in 30 days or so, you probably are not going to; toss it, or file it. If you get something that you need to read before a future meeting, wait to read it until just before the meeting; do not read it as soon as you get it. Put it in your "Hold" file, and note the date to read it on your calendar (Winston, 81). If part of your job is going through the newspaper, just skim the headlines. Read only the stories you need to read, and save the funnies for lunchtime.

If you use public transit or are in a carpool, your daily commute is a great time to catch up on your reading. Other good times are while you are waiting for a computer file to load, defragging, or backing up your files. The taxi ride to a meeting is also an opportunity to go over materials or your presentation.

Technology

Machines should work. People should think.

An IBM slogan (in Griessman, 193)

Technology is wonderful, but it is not quite the answer to all our problems. In fact, it often creates problems of its own. Consider the time it takes to select the right equipment, learn to use it (a real time sink), arrange to fix it when it breaks—which it inevitably will—or fix it yourself, and the time lost while it is out of service. Before you okay that purchase order, ask yourself if you really *need* that new gadget or piece of software. Never upgrade just because there's something new. And when you get it, resist the temptation to try to learn everything about it right away. Look through the manual to find out what the equipment or program can do, but learn the details on the features as you need them. If your computer "doesn't do what you need, don't just gripe. Instead, write up in detail what you need, why you need it, and how it will pay off for the company" (Aslett, 57). Pekka Himanen, philosophy researcher at the University of Helsinki, Finland (Debra Wood, 50), says:

> Another way to gain the upper hand on technology is to wrest control from the gadgets. Just because technology makes a task possible doesn't mean you always have to take advantage of it. In this connected time, it's very important to disconnect oneself from time to time so as to get some distance and be able to rise above just reacting to immediate things. In those peaceful moments one can thing bigger, slower, and about more inner questions without which we aren't human, but simply survivors

Learn basic computer troubleshooting skills so that you do not have to wait for someone to come to fix the computer. It is not professional, when you have a computer down and an angry customer, to say, "That's not my job," "The computer people will have to fix it," or "I don't know what to do." Speaking of learning, Pedley (4) says:

> It is well worth spending time with your users providing training, whether on the online databases that they have access to from their desktops; the Internet; or on the resources that are available through

your Intranet pages. Help the users to become more self-sufficient so
that they are able to find the answers to quick questions for themselves

You may have to make some changes in the way you learn, too. "I
think my primary way of learning—from way back in school—is a
combination of diving into something on my own and being able to
lean over and ask a nearby expert how to do a certain task. I've turned
to using customer help desks when available. I have had to put aside
time for on-site training when possible" (a corporate librarian).

What good is a computer, after all? "You have to figure out what
you want to do and then find out how you can use a computer to auto-
mate the process. *You* have to do it—nobody else can" (Jeffrey Mayer,
efficiency expert, in Lamont Wood, 26). The computer is wonderful for
some things. For instance:

- Mailing lists
- Financial records
- Automating repetitive tasks
- Storing information from business cards! You can search for information much faster because there are multiple entry points
  (name, company, where you met, type of business, location, and so
  on)

Perhaps the best use for a computer is keeping sets of boilerplate files.
Store any document you might use again on your computer. This includes, but is not limited to the following:

- Common answers to common questions, headers, references, order
  forms, loan requests, your commercial, and so on.
- Addresses you use frequently. Use a label- or envelope-addressing
  program. You can even preprint labels for addresses you use often.
  Try a special label printer (Seiko© and Dymo© make good ones)
  for creating one or two address labels. It is much faster than load-
  ing a whole sheet of labels.
- Keep an index or directory of your boilerplate files, or make a
  short list of them (a cheat sheet) and keep it by your computer.
- For reports you write regularly, make a standard form. Keep the
  most recent form on the computer, and just change what you need
  to: dates and numbers. It is also a good way to make sure you follow up on what you said last time.

- Use a preprinted (or boilerplate on the computer) fax cover sheet. Fax stickers save space, but have to be filled in every time and are hard to read.
- Use preprinted routing and referral forms. Include names, subject, date, from, and action requested (FYI, Let's discuss, Please handle, Call me, Return, and so on).
- A computerized address book is definitely superior to paper. It may not be as portable, but you can print it out or use a PDA. You can transfer your paper address book or Rolodex to the computer or use it to backup the paper one on the computer. You can then carry one copy and have one safely back home in the office. (It is also a good idea to have one copy at home in case your employment is terminated suddenly.)

Here are some other tips and techniques for more time-efficient use of a computer. Treat the files on your computer just like paper files. Delete old ones, send some on to others, file some on floppies or other remote storage, and back them up. I cannot stress this enough—BACK UP, BACK UP, BACK UP!!! I find that most people do not back up their hard drive until it has crashed at least twice, taking your data with it. Also, clean up your hard drive regularly. Schedule—right now—a time to clean up your hard drive, reorganize what is left, and back it up. Do not scan anything you would not save anyway. Write down success-ful search strategies and databases to use next time. Label all computer disks and files completely and logically. Call your file "letter to John Doe," not "jd1." (This is especially easy now that most programs allow for long filenames.) Color-code computer disks. Put the filename, path, date, and time in the header or footer of printed documents, especially those with numbers or calculations. *Always* date spreadsheets. Use "find and replace," "auto correct," or "auto text" (or whatever your program calls these features). For instance, type "SF" then later replace it with "Santa Fe, New Mexico." Use a recipe box and 3-by-5 cards for passwords and short instructions, and put the box by your computer (Foust, Part 2, 25). Always carry two batteries for your laptop com-puter. You may not have access to an outlet. For long trips, a battery charger is very handy.

Finally, here are two great ideas for using technology, both from a German academic librarian:

I find all possibilities of a homepage or an Intranet very instructive for colleagues and clients, things like FAQ-lists and so on. [However,] these sites should *always* be supplemented with mailing lists or newsgroups to push information to those who want it.

I've created a web-page with all the addresses I often use, loaded it on my home page and made it the "home" of my browser. If I want to write a letter to my director, for example, I only need to click on the "home" button and then click on the address of the director and I have the e-mail-window with address, a notation on the subject line that it is the library writing to him and in the body the correct form of address. Take advantage of the possibilities of the "mail-to" Tag in HTML: (<a href="mailto:prename.name@organization.net"> prename.name@organization.net</a>): You then can just click on a [sic] e-mail-address at the web page and an e-mail-window opens with this exact e-mail-address. You can expand the tag with notations about the subject and text of the body. For example:
<a href="mailtoprename.name@organization.net?subject=[OPL-Address-Pool]&body=Dear Mr. name, prename.name@organization.net > </a.

The Telephone

Today we do a lot of communicating by telephone. Although it may be faster to use the telephone rather than go somewhere, telephone calls can be a large factor in wasting time when not handled properly. Do not allow the telephone to run your life. You do *not* have to answer it every time it rings. In fact, you shouldn't, especially when you have someone in your office or when you need to concentrate on something, such as an online search or major report. You are the master; the telephone is your slave. You should use the answering machine or voice mail when you are working on a rush project, when a project requires all your attention, or when a customer is in front of you. Voice mail that takes a message even when you are on the telephone is definitely preferable to an answering machine that only answers when you are out of the office.

Never pick up someone else's telephone. If you do, you will inherit that person's problem.

Answer the telephone with your name and the name of the organization or library. Be prepared to repeat yourself, because most people really will not listen to your greeting.

There is nothing worse than not reaching the person you want, unless it is reaching a poor message on an answering machine. And, there is nothing better than reaching a good message. What's the difference? A good answering machine message will give the caller a brief but clear message and then encourage him or her to leave a detailed message. Ideally, it will give you the time and date of the call automatically (rather than relying on the caller to do so). The message you record should clearly identify your library, you, or both. The message also should be business-like (save the cute messages for your home machine). If you are out of the office for a day or more, the message should say when you will return and what to do or whom to call in the meantime. If you are just busy or on the phone, the message should say something such as: "I'm sorry that I can't help you right now, but I am currently serving another patron. Please leave a detailed message with your information need, and I will get back to you as soon as I can." (This says that you care about the client's question, are working with someone else, and will return the call. I recently heard a recording that said, "All our service representatives are busy giving someone else the personal attention you will receive shortly. Thank you for your patient understanding." I really like this message.) Give callers an option other than leaving a message, such as another person to call if the situation is urgent. Listen to your greeting occasionally and make sure it is still appropriate.

Check your machine frequently, and return calls religiously and as soon as possible. The person is more likely to still be available. Get in the habit of checking your messages as soon as you return to your desk. If your machine takes messages while you are on the phone, check it each time you hang up. You want to become known for answering messages promptly so that customers will not be reluctant to leave messages for you. (This is also true of your e-mail!) Use a duplicate message pad. Transfer voice-mail or answering-machine messages to the pad. Have a pen by the phone; ensure that it will not walk away by putting it on a cord or chain (Allen, 74). "Try returning telephone calls about ten minutes before lunchtime or ten minutes before the end of the day. Most people are in their offices at these times (Pollar, 166) or, if you just want to leave a message and do not need (or want) conversation, call at other times, such as at lunchtime. When leaving a telephone message, speak clearly and distinctly. Be brief and to the point. Do not ramble. Give your full name and telephone number early in the message, in case you run out of recording time. Repeat your telephone number for clarity.

What about the cell phone? Personally, I refuse to have one. I just do not care to be that connected. But many people feel that they must have one or are required to have one by their managers. Cell phones can be time savers, especially when you need further instructions or directions on the way to an appointment. (But if you reconfirm an appointment before you leave, you shouldn't need to call on the road—unless you are delayed by traffic.) There has been a lot written about cell telephone etiquette. Practice the golden rule: Treat others as you would have them treat you. Do not take or make cell telephone calls during a meeting, an appointment, a concert or play, in a restaurant, or on public transportation. If you *must* be on constant call, get a pager that can be set to vibrate silently. Then call the person back when you are able to do so privately. You would be amazed how many people talk about confidential matters on cell phones. You never know who might be listening to your conversation—it could be a competitor of your company.

Finally, here are some more good telephone time management tips. "Keep a 'hot list' of important but not often called numbers by each telephone so you can find them in a hurry if needed" (Tomlin, 8). An idea I got from the beauty shop is to put the telephone number by the person's name in your appointment book (or on your calendar) so you can call if a delay occurs of if you need directions. Put a list of all key contacts in the project file, with telephone numbers (Aslett, 93). "Circle or highlight telephone numbers the first time you look up each number in the telephone directory. You are very likely to need it again" (Pollar, 43).

Here are some hints for cutting off a long-winded person. At an opening ask, "Now, what can I do for you?" You also can tell the caller you are on your way to a meeting and just have a minute, or say you have someone in the office so you must be quick.

Straighten your desk, check e-mail, or open mail (or do something) while you are on hold.

Try a telephone headset, cordless phone, or cell phone. Use the special features on your phone: caller ID, memory dial, long cord, re-dial, headset, speakerphone, voice mail, voice-activated dialing, call forwarding, and call waiting. In many parts of the United States, you can use some of these only when you need them, at extra cost. "We have a portable phone, this means we can provide service to clients full time during operating hours, can walk to the stacks to answer a question while still talking to a client, don't have to waste time running between stacks and phone" (head of a Canadian government library).

"Don't take calls from publishers' reps, only return them" (Australian law librarian).

Other Office Hints

"One company took an idea from the airlines when it installed a light above the copier that could be seen by the entire office. When the light was on, people knew the equipment was in use and could avoid an unnecessary walk (Allen, 55).

Tape equipment manuals to the side of the equipment (Aslett, 103), but keep a copy in a file for when that one disappears. If there is a warranty or service contract, make a note on your calendar for one month before it expires. Try to get the machine checked, serviced, and cleaned now while it is free.

If a fax is important, call the recipient to let him or her know it is coming. The fax machine may not be nearby or even turned on.

When you take the next to last of something, put it on a buy list, then you will not have to make a rush trip or order.

Buy quality, not by price. It is often less expensive in the long run because it saves time in repairs or having to buy a replacement sooner.

When sending information to a client, add a quick, simple feedback form ("Is this what you wanted? Did it help? Is there anything else I can do for you?") or jot a note on your calendar to send one in, say, one week.

Keep things such as your federal tax ID number in your Rolodex (Pollar, 39).

Always process money or related correspondence immediately and get it to the bank, before you lose it (Aslett, 90).

Vow to eliminate at least one form right now, then look for another, and another. . . .

Always sign your full name on memos and date them, including the year (Aslett, 83). On memos, Guy St. Clair (1993) writes: "If you don't need a permanent record of the interaction, use the phone. If there is room for misunderstanding, write a memo. If you need a written response, write. If you need to talk to more than one person, write rather than call." When writing a report, first make sure that it will serve a purpose. Do not write reports that will not be read.

"Keep track of what you do! I have a database that I have kept for 11 years of all the requests I've received. By running through a document number or title I can refer requestors to others interested in the same information. I think this is informal knowledge management and has proved useful to me and others" (a corporate librarian).

Filing

Many librarians are great paper shufflers, for good reason. Librarians are trained to organize and place material where it can be retrieved at some time in the future. Because that is their professional training, librarians can carry it to an extreme.

J. Wesley Cochran

Almost everyone dislikes filing—me included. (I usually do not file until either the box is overflowing onto the floor or I have been through it three times looking for something. Again, do as I say, not as I do.) Filing is a great time-wasting activity if not done right.

The object of filing is not to store things, but to be able to find them when you need them. "Think 'retrieval system' not 'filing system,'" says author and organizing consultant Hope Lafferty of (S)PACE in Austin, Texas. Think about where you will look for the information, not where you got it or what the report or article might be called. Use the broadest categories possible. What pops into your head when you look at the file? That is often your best label, according to Judith Kolberg, founder of the National Study Group for Chronic Disorganization (NSGCD) (Turner). Corcoran (218) goes even further—"Don't save it if you can't find it later!" Experts estimate that between 80 and 95 percent of everything filed is never looked at again. However, filing is critical. "The average executive wastes 150 hours per year looking for lost, misplaced, misfiled, or mislabeled documents" (Coopers & Lybrand survey, 1976, www.123sortit.com, Paper Files). In 1996, *Office World News* estimated the average cost to file a paper document at $30, to find a misfiled document at $20, and to recreate a lost document at $250 (www.123sortit.com, Paper Files). These numbers undoubtedly are even higher now.

Where on earth do you find time to file? Here are two great suggestions from librarians. "I once took a class on getting organized, and the best tip that I remember is that it's too difficult to sort and file at the same time. First sort items, then file them. Of course best of all is to handle something only once and not have piles that need to be sorted" (librarian in a not-for-profit organization). Pedley (4) says:

Whilst I try not to take work home with me, one thing that I certainly find useful is to take a pile of papers home with me. I then spend time listening to the radio or watching the television whilst sorting through the paperwork. Librarians seem to hoard material; they always seem to be reluctant to throw anything away. Be ruthless, as you go through your paperwork, throw as much material away as you can.

Then with what remains, sort it into themes. Now that you have gathered together batches of paperwork organised by theme, the next step is to sort the themes out in order of importance

You can do only 4½ things with any piece of information:

    1.   Toss it.
    2.   Refer it.
    3.   Act on it.
    4.   File it.
    4½. Read it.

To decide which of these applies, use "logic-based disposal":

- Does it require action on my part? If not, toss it or file it.
- Does it exist elsewhere? If so (and it is easy to get to), toss it.
- Is it outdated? If so, toss it.
- Will it become obsolete before I need it again?
- Will I *really* use it again? If not, toss it. Do not use "just in case" logic.
- Are there tax or legal implications? If so, file it.
- What is the worst thing that could happen if I do not have this information? If you can live with the answer, toss it.
- Does anyone else need this information? If so, file it or give it to them.

Clark and Clark (120) list three categories of items that you should never file:

1. *Routine memos:* read them, take action, remember them, toss them.
2. *Meeting announcements:* write the dates on your calendar, then toss them.
3. *Company information on file somewhere else:* Isn't it nice when someone else keeps things for you?

You need to create a record-retention policy if you do not already have one. You should follow your parent organization's policy if there is one. If you need help, contact your legal or financial officer, an accountant, or a records manager. Here is one example of what a policy should look like (Tolpa):

Keep indefinitely:
    Annual financial statements
    Corporate board documents
    Things that are irreplaceable or expensive to recreate
Keep as long as owned or being depreciated:
    Information on capital purchases
Keep 7 years:
    Income tax paperwork
    Checks
Keep 6 years:
    Bank statements
    Voided checks
    Purchase and sales records
Keep 4 years:
    Personnel records
    Payroll records
Keep 3 years:
    Monthly financial statements
    Current projects (Allen, 77)

Here are some suggestions from www.123sortit.com, Paper Files:

- "When naming files, always stick with the first identifying name that comes to mind.
- Title folders with a noun, not an adjective (Lists, not New Lists).
- Label files not by where they came from or what they are, but by the next action required—telephone calls to make; checks, letters, or purchase orders to write; items to look up; items to take to a meeting (with a separate folder for each meeting); or things to read.
- When you have a minute you can just pull something from the 'Telephone call' file, or the 'To-read' file, or whatever."

Other possible categories for files are by client, chronological, tickler (either 31-day or rolling), or travel (1 file per trip). Some people have a chronological file, usually a copy. This works well with correspondence. Nutty suggests the 43 Tickler File System. This consists of 31 folders representing each day of the current month and 12 folders representing each month (1 = January, 2 = February, and so on). You use it as follows. It is now October 10. You have two items. One must be done on October 20, and the other is due December 15. Put information on the first item in the "20" folder. Put the other in the "December" folder. The items in the 31 folders are for October, so when you get to the 20th you will have the information ready to work on. On December

1, take the contents of the "12" folder (December) and distribute them to the 31 daily folders. When it is December 15, you will find that information in the "15" folder.

You should also make a file for each project—as soon as you start the project. After the project is finished, throw out duplicates and preliminary information. Keep everything related to decisions, legal issues, or money. Replace any paper clips with staples. "Note and file any lessons you learned in completing" the project (Stanley Smith, 43). (This is especially true of mistakes; no one reports failures but you learn the most from failures.) Move the cleaned-out file to dead or off-site storage.

Speaking of off-site storage, label all boxes on all four sides (www.123sortit.com, Paper Files) and write the purge date on the front. Corcoran (203) suggests having hot and cold files: hot for this week, cold for inactive projects.

Have a miscellaneous or "Don't know where to file" file. Go through it regularly. File an item when you think of the right place to put it or when there is enough of one topic to make a new folder.

"Most businesses . . . have a human filing convention," not a written one. If that person leaves it is difficult to find things (Allen, 64). Therefore, it is very important to make an index to your files. The best place to keep this is in the front of each file cabinet (not drawer). Be sure to keep a second copy somewhere (such as in a file labeled "Index to files") or on the computer.

File *at least* weekly. Even better, refile items when you are through with them and file every day—or at least file the important stuff. So that you know where to file something, write a key word on the item when you read it, before you put it in your filing tray—especially if someone else does your filing. It is also a good idea to put a purge date—the date to discard the information—on the piece of paper at the same time.

File according to how you will use it, not where it came from. Judy's first law of filing: If you have trouble finding something in the files, put it back where you first looked for it (or at least put a pointer sheet there). If something is too large to go into a file, put a pointer to it in the file, for example, "Training video on top shelf of bookcase." Jasper suggests filing papers "according to what you'll use them for, not where they came from or what they are" (Jasper, 115).

Always put a folder back immediately after using it. Put a marker of some sort in the location from which you take a file folder. Special "out" cards are available that ask for the name and office location of the person taking the file, or you can make your own marker.

Always file the most recent information in the front of the folder. Use staples rather than paper clips to avoid items getting stuck together. Use manila subfolders within hanging files so that when you take the information out, you leave the file in its proper place. Make sure the interior folder is labeled with the folder name. Put tabs on hanging files in the *front*—they are easier to see when the file is full. Purge your files at the same time as you file. If you always file the newest information in the font, it is easy to purge from the back. As a file gets thick, go through it and delete or divide.

Here are some miscellaneous filing tips:

- Never file envelopes unless the postmark is significant—put addresses in your Rolodex or on a computer file.
- If multiple people access the files, have only *one* person do the refiling to minimize errors.
- Do not put business cards in books, which are difficult to alphabetize, find things in, and change. Staple them to a large Rolodex card or file them in a special business-card-sized file. Better yet, use a contact manager such as Act!®
- Always use logical file names, and type the file name at the top of the first page of the document.
- Vertical file cabinets are more versatile, hold more, take up less space, are easier to use, and are less expensive than lateral files. Lateral files are better for narrow spaces and if you file while you are sitting down, and they provide added counter space. If you file or access files sitting down, do not put high-use files in the top drawer or use lateral files.
- Use color to distinguish between types of files.
- Keep all forms together, regardless of subject. You might even want to do the same for reports and statistics.
- For infrequently asked questions that have difficult-to-find answers, put sources on a Rolodex card for the next time the question is asked.
- Prioritize assignments by placing a colored Post-it note on each one with the due date or date to do it (a few days before the due date).

The Mail

A librarian in a not-for-profit organization says:

In the interest of efficiency my organization did away with mail delivery personnel. I am now my own mail person. I have a bag that
contains my periodical check-in cards, a stapler, a pencil and preprinted routing slips. When I'm in the mailroom, I go through the
mail there, tossing and sorting into piles and checking in periodicals
and attaching routing slips and putting them right back into the mail
slots rather than taking the mail back to my area and doing those
tasks there.

This is a wonderful idea!

If you cannot deal with your mail in the mail room, follow the
same procedure in your office. Open the mail and sort it over the
wastebasket. Throw out junk mail immediately, unread. (However, I
have found that most librarians at least *look* at anything new, even junk
mail. Some junk mail is informative so do not be too quick to judge it.)
Decide on each piece of paper as it comes in, but do it quickly. Do not
waste too much time on this. Winston says to spend no more than an
hour a day on mail—this seems high to me. Put bills in your "To pay"
folder. Put requests in your "Action" folder. Refer what you can to
someone else. Put lengthy items in your "To read" folder.

To get off junk mailing lists, write the publisher or the company, or
(in the United States) request a Mail Preference Form from

> Mail Preference Service
> c/o Direct Marketing Association
> PO Box 9008
> Farmingdale, NY 11735

Use overnight delivery only if it is a matter of life and death and
the recipient is willing to pay for it. (You can almost always avoid this
by not waiting until the last minute.)

When dealing with interlibrary loans (ILLs), Tomlin suggests that
you remove "mailing labels from the original packaging, re-label for
the return trip, and mark with the ILL number *before* distributing the
items. Unless damaged, reuse the same boxes or bags the ILLs came
in" (Tomlin, 9).

E-Mail

E-mail is the oxygen of the Internet. But used badly, it can smother recipients and slow down an entire company. Using e-mail effectively is what separates the savvy manager from those who don't get it.

Mark Breier and Armin A. Brott

We all know that librarians need to keep in touch with their colleagues and customers. Electronic discussion lists and e-mail are two excellent ways to do this. However, you can spend—and waste—a lot of time on e-mail. Here are some tips for managing your e-mail. I have divided them into outgoing (sending e-mail) and incoming (reading and storing e-mail). At the end are some good general suggestions from a librarian and from the giant high-tech corporation Intel.

Do the following for outgoing e-mail:

- Put the subject and *desired action* in the subject line. Be clear. Be concise (three paragraphs as a maximum).
- Do not copy people who do not really need to see the message. Add value (a note or a comment) when forwarding.
- Make macros or boilerplates for e-mail. Simply make a file with the repeated information and import or copy it into your outgoing message.
- "After the third e-mail on the same subject, walk 'n talk." This is sometimes called the Three Strikes Rule. Do not waste any more time talking by e-mail—do it face to face (Breier and Brott, 54).

Do the following for incoming e-mail:

- Use an e-mail program that filters or sorts messages into files or folders, such as Eudora Pro® (not the free, light version). That way you can read the important stuff first. I sort by source—where it came from, especially for messages from electronic lists.
- Triage by source and subject fields, without opening the messages themselves.
- Reduce junk mail by going to The National Waste Prevention Coalition site at www.metrokc.gov/nwpc and clicking on "Reduce Business Junk Mail" (St. James, 53).
- Read electronic lists at home. If you find something you want to save, send it by e-mail to yourself at work. "Get a separate [e-mail] account for your personal stuff." The company account will remain

archived in the company and can come back to haunt you (Breier and Brott, 56).

- Some experts say not to print out messages and clutter your desk with them. I disagree. Print them and file them like anything else. However, be sure to do as Tolpa says: "Think before you print." Is it valuable? Will you really read it? If not, bookmark it instead.
- As with regular mail, try to handle messages only once. TRAF still applies; either Toss (delete) it, Refer (forward) it, Answer it, or File it.
- Keep e-mail in your in-box until you are ready to reply so that you will not forget.
- Check e-mail remotely if you will be gone for a while; it saves time when you get back. Or, have it forwarded to someone else to look at for you. Get off lists before you leave or set to no-mail.
- Do not subscribe to electronic lists in the digest version because it actually takes *longer* to go through the whole digest. Also, if you want to save just one of the messages, you have to cut and paste. It is very fast to just delete messages.

Keep your e-mail files clean. "Schedule a time—maybe the first of each month—for deleting piled up e-mail you haven't answered and never will" (St. James, 57). Delete messages you have responded to—they are in your out box anyway. Make a file of things to keep, and go through it regularly. Purge folders and out/delete files regularly. If it has been a couple of months, you probably do not need it. One major exception is addresses. File them somewhere if you think you might ever use them again. They are too hard to track down. I have a separate folder labeled "Addresses to save" and purge it regularly for ones no longer of use. Eisenberg (192) suggests making a list of your e-mail addresses and putting it in your regular address book so you can keep in touch away from the office. A Chicago librarian suggests that you "automatically save all sent mail and store in folders by month. I need only to remember about when something happened and I can retrieve the message I sent you about it. If you've forgotten or didn't read it, I can send it back to you. Also, since I always include the original message in my reply, I can retrieve the message you sent me, even if I never filed the original."

Check e-mail regularly, but only at specific times. I check it at 9 a.m., 1 p.m., and 4 p.m. Some experts say to check it only once a day, but that just is not enough. If you are an e-mail "junkie," try checking it only "on the hour." No one will think you are a slacker if you get back to them within the hour" (Jackie Edmondson in Abernathy, 25).

If you can, turn off that little beep that tells you that you have e-mail.

"The biggest problems most business have are from not listening to customers, not focusing on customer service, and not working hard to understand what customers want. The Internet offers tremendous opportunities to solicit and receive customer feedback" (Breier and Brott, 14–15). To get feedback by e-mail, set up an anonymous, electronic question or suggestion box. Jeff Bezos of Amazon.com agrees. "E-mail turns off the politeness gene in human beings. People are more willing to be rude and truthful by e-mail than they ever would be in person or over the phone. For a company [or library], that's wonderful" (in Anders).

A Canadian medical librarian tells how to prioritize e-mail and make it count:

1. "If a copy of something is sent to me, it gets filed in a folder marked 'not read' since it was probably sent just for the record anyway.
2. If you want more than one person to read what you send, mark it high priority and put the name of the high-priority person at the top of the list (forget alphabetical order).
3. Make a habit of using your 'sent' file as an e-record of your work and include it in your statistical report."

Here are Intel's 10 Commandments of E-mail (Overholt):

1. Don't use your in-box as a catchall folder for everything you need to work on.
2. Create a "Five Weeks" folder that deletes its contents automatically after five weeks.
3. Assist colleagues' in-box-filtering efforts by agreeing on acronyms to use in subject lines that identify important messages.
4. Send group mail only when it is useful to all recipients.
5. Ask to be removed from distribution lists that you don't need to be on.
6. Traveling? Use your e-mail's "out-of-office" feature. [Caution: Don't do this if you are on electronic lists. There is little more annoying than receiving a lot of "out-of-office" messages after you post to a list.]
7. When possible, send a message that is only a subject line, so recipients don't have to open the e-mail to read a single line. End the subject line with <EOM>, the acronym for End of Message.

8. Use graphics and attachments sparingly. [and *never* send attachments to lists]
9. Put attachments larger than 5 MB on the company's Web site or Intranet.
10. Be specific. If you send a 20-page attachment, tell the recipient that the important information is on pages 2 and 17.

Your Calendar

Used properly, your calendar or date book can be a powerful time management tool. Not only will it help you remember meetings and appointments, but other important things as well. Write down things that you need to follow-up on, such as "Call John back," or "Check on the progress of project X." You can also write down personal deadlines—clean out files, run a current awareness search for an important client. In the section on managing your to-read pile, I suggested you not read reports for a meeting until just before the meeting date. On your calendar, put a note for three days or so before the meeting to "Read report for meeting on the 12th." Do not forget to use the calendar for due dates for repetitive tasks, such as monthly reports, return dates for ILLs, or even important telephone calls to be made.

What kind of calendar should you use? Use whatever feels comfortable and works for you. I have used different kinds at different times in different ways. The two-pages-per-day type is great for daily reminders or to-do lists (more on to-do lists in the next section). I used the blank side to keep track of what I accomplished each day. This made it much easier to write my monthly report. The desk-blotter size is great for seeing a whole month at a glance. It makes it easy to see what is coming up and to check quickly for potential conflicts. I use a yearly pocket calendar as my master calendar. Everything goes in this one—professional, personal, travel, birthdays, even my husband's schedule. If it is not in the pocket calendar, it will not get done.

Of course, no calendar works if you do not put a meeting or appointment date on the calendar as soon as you know the date—even if it is tentative. It is crucial that you have one and only one master calendar. If you must have another portable one, but be sure to enter dates into the master immediately on returning to the office. If you use an electronic calendar, back it up regularly. If you have a secretary or assistant, make sure he or she has access to your calendar. You can even use his or her copy as your backup. Give yourself the gift of time. Sit down; train co-workers not to disturb you or go somewhere you ill not be bothered. Check in with your goals, projects, and weekly events.

Block out time for what is important. Schedule like items together. Write it all down. Use this time to give yourself structure so that you can be spontaneous when opportunity knocks.

Your To-Do List

Without a [to-do] list, you can get caught up in trivial, useless, dead-end stuff. Before you know it, the day's over and you wonder, 'Where did the time go? I didn't get anything worthwhile done today.'

Lee Silber

Do not start the day wondering what will "happen" today—have a plan. But a to-do list should be like a recipe is to a good cook—only a guideline, an outline—not a set of requirements carved in stone. That is, the world will not come to an end if everything does not get done. Do not let yourself become a slave to your to-do list. "Leave things undone if you can live with the consequences. But *choose* to leave them undone"—not just because your forgot them (Silber, 134). Be willing to make *necessary* exceptions to your plan.

Weeks (42–44) writes that there are three must-be's, three should-be's, and three may-be's for to-do lists:

- *Must-be's:* daily, written, and prioritized.
- *Should-be's:* no more than 10 items, kept in the same place, and written at the end of the day.
- *May-be's:* written however you choose, changed as needed, and used as a form of communication (and discipline).

Write your to-do list with the three most important items first. Bly suggests working on the most important one first until done, then the next, and so on. But this is probably unrealistic for most librarians. Just do the best you can. When you are interrupted, take care of the interruption, then go back to the top three. If you carry a to-do list with you at all times, you can easily write down ideas when they occur. Deciding what to do and what not to do is critical. This requires continually checking your mission statement. Eliminate things from your to-do list by asking yourself: What is the worst that can happen if I *do not* do this? If you can live with this, delete it. Am I the only person who can do this? If not, delegate it. Must it be done now? If not, put it aside and reconsider it later. (It might go away.) Is there an easier way to do it? If so, do it that way.

Break your day into segments of no more than one hour. Scheduling tasks into one-hour slots gives you a deadline to do your task—one hour. But leave time for larger projects as well. "In building each day's schedule, librarians should not overlook the fact, though, that they owe themselves the same courtesy given others—their time and undivided attention. [Schedule] some time each day to concentrate on those tasks that you have identified as a high-priority" (Cochran, 25). Library managers may want to review each employee's own daily to-do list, but the manager should not dictate. He or she should let employees compile their own list.

Nutty suggests organizing your to-do list like this. Make a list of tasks. Assign a value to each, where A means vital (life- or job-threatening); B means important; and C is for tasks that are fast, fun or friendly. Priority C tasks can be substituted when you *cannot* do an A or B task or as fill-ins or when you need a list or reward. Your list will then look like this.

Action Priority	Task
A	
A	
B	

In the action column, you can insert one of the following symbols:

$\Rightarrow$ An item that you could not get done and have moved ahead or to another list.

3   Completed.

5   Canceled. (You decided not to do this task.)

JAS   Delegated to someone else. (Enter the initials of the person to whom you delegated the task.)

Here are some suggestions for your to-do list from a solo librarian:

- Never put more than five things on it.
- At the end of each day, write down three to four worthwhile things you have done that day.
- At the end of the day, write down the five things you want to do to start the next day.
- Have it on your desk, so you see it first thing in the morning. The first hour of your workday is the most important.

When should you write your to-do list? There are two options—choose the one that works best for you. You can do it at the beginning or end of every day. I suggest that you do it at the end of the day when there are usually fewer interruptions and distractions. "Before you leave work [check your desk to make sure you haven't missed something important, and], make a to-do list of no more than five items that you hope to accomplish the following day. This simple procedure will give you closure at the end of the day, as well as get you focused when you arrive the next morning" (Bacon). This also allows you to go over what you accomplished (write these down on your calendar or somewhere for your periodic reports). Be sure to take a minute and pat yourself on the back, too. Finally, post the list by your desk or on your computer where you will see it first thing in the morning, put on your coat, and go home!

You should also have a long-term to-do list. This master list should include *everything* you have to do, want to do, or dream of doing. Use it to make your daily to-do list, adding in any urgent tasks that have come up and scheduled items taken from your calendar.

What kind of planner should you use? Just as with calendars, the choice is up to you. The most common types follow:

- Date books, usually showing one week or month at a time.
- Appointment books, with hour-by-hour listings.
- Planners, such as Filofax®, DayTimer®, Franklin®, Day Runner®, Rolodex®, Keith Clark®, Cambridge®, At-a-Glance®, and Planner Pad®.
- Electronic planners or software for desktop and laptop computers, personal information managers (PIMs), or personal digital assistants (PDAs).

Neither paper nor electronic is best for everyone. If you like gadgets, and feel confident about using technology-based solutions, you might want to invest in a hand-held organizer. These devices, also known as PDAs, are easy to carry and are evolving into extremely powerful tools. If you are a more tactile person who likes a written format, stick with a paper-based planner. If you write large and take many notes, you might choose a planner with a larger letter size or a legal-sized planner (Turner). Paper and electronic systems each have pros and cons. Paper is portable, is always accessible, requires a short data-entry time, is not dependent on electricity, is unlikely to be stolen (since it has no intrinsic value to others), and is inexpensive. The down side is that you must manually transfer tasks and dates from one day, month, or year. Electronic planners make for easier rescheduling: you can set recurring events and unfinished tasks are automatically carried over to the next day. Electronic planners are easily searchable and can be portable by transferring them to a PDA. The down side is that electronic planners are expensive, have a relatively long learning curve, may crash, are dependent on power, may have a small keyboard (PDAs) and be hard to read, are vulnerable to theft, and take time to boot up.

Here are examples of how three librarians use their to-do lists and planners. A librarian in a not-for-profit organization says:

> I try and group tasks if possible and do them on specific days: cataloging on Fridays, shelving returned items on Tuesdays, etc. Of course, many is the time I have had the day set aside for technical processing chores and a reference project lands on my desk and takes preference.

Pedley (4) says:

> I spend time trying to think through what are the key action points that I need to deal with. I make a list of these, and then I make sure that I have the appropriate piles of supporting documentation organised in the same order as the list of tasks to be done. I always find that this saves me a considerable amount of time. It means that I don't end up having to spend hours at work just sifting through piles of paperwork to find the required background information. Even if you have made a list of the tasks that you want to complete that day, you have to accept that life isn't always quite so straightforward. You may be called to a meeting at short notice, an urgent enquiry might take precedence over everything else, or you [may] get so many telephone calls that you don't get a spare moment to begin working through your list.

A librarian in an information research firm says:

> I've used the Day Timer® one-page-a-day Senior Pocket format since the 1960s. This has basically been used in reverse. I've always just marked in what I have done when, and then go back and look. I've been able to see what I'm spending most of my time on and can extrapolate from that whether I'm spending too much time on nonessential things. It has also proven to be a good "proof of service," i.e., it tells the bosses that I do indeed do something. At one point I was able to show that what was required for a half-time job actually took 39 hours a week and I was given a very large raise. And I could categorize the processes that took that much time, to help the board see the need for help, which I then received.

Business Travel

Nearly all librarians have to travel for business from time to time. Travel can waste a large quantity of time if not planned for adequately. First, try to avoid traveling at all. Use the telephone or e-mail instead of going somewhere for a meeting. Can you have the other participants come to you, or can someone else go instead? Try to group appointments or visits to nearby cities.

If you *must* go, make a checklist to save on preparation time and to avoid forgetting things. Make multiple copies and use the list every time you travel. Arrange to have your work taken care of while you are away—or at least make sure the important tasks get done. If you do not have an assistant to take care of your mail, at least have someone collect it every day and put it in a secure location. This will keep your users from going through the mail and taking items out (that you will never know came in). Leave a clear message on your voice mail stating when you will return. (If you are going to a professional conference or continuing education opportunity, be sure to say something such as, "I am in Chicago to attend a training workshop so I will be able to fulfill your information needs better." This reminds them of your professionalism.)

Many people like to work on the airplane. However, I think this is a wonderful time to relax and think about your career, goals, and aspirations. You will frequently have one of those aha! moments when the solution to a sticky work problem becomes crystal clear. Work only when you *have* to—and you should not have to if you have planned the trip well. You can always work at the hotel.

Speaking of the hotel, make sure that it has a business center, with e-mail, fax, and shipping services. If you must work in your room, ask if there is a room with Internet access or a fax machine. Be sure to ask the cost of these services. It may be less expensive to find an Internet café nearby. You might find that using room service for some meals can save you valuable time, especially on the day of your departure. You can get ready to leave, not spend time sitting in a crowded restaurant. Just remember that you are paying for saved time with spent money.

I take my laptop along and make notes each evening of what I did and with whom I spoke. This makes it much easier to write a trip report—which should be done *as soon as* you return.

Here is one last hint that can save you a lot of time. If your flight is canceled or delayed, do not stand in line waiting to see the desk agent. Go directly to a telephone (or use your cell phone if you have one) and call the reservations line to make your change. You will be rebooked while others are still waiting to talk to the desk agent.

Conferences

If your manager is not another librarian (and perhaps he or she is), one of the most difficult issues is how to convince him or her to send you to a professional association conference. Tomlin (8) suggests that you "point out that you can get a greater number of continuing education credits by spending less than a week at a national conference once a year than by sporadic absences for fewer credits over twelve months." Personally, I suspect part of our problem is that upper management's conferences are far less learning-intensive than ours. If they went to just one library conference and saw how hard we work at learning, talking to vendors, and networking, there would never be a problem with getting permission again.

Before you go, write out a ranked list of your objectives for the conference. You will probably do this when preparing your request to your boss for funding. Contact people you need to meet before the conference to confirm a time and place to meet. When the conference offers too many conflicting sessions or events, find a colleague who also is attending and split your list with him or her. After the conference you can get together and exchange notes. Take along any tough reference questions you have (or sample questions) so that you can use them to try out vendors' products (and get free answers). Also take a notebook, pens and pencils, tape, paper clips, some file folders, and highlighter pens (to mark your program).

I always go through the preliminary program and make a tentative schedule of sessions. Don't forget to plan to go to the various vendor and association parties. Be sure to call them "networking opportunities" when talking to nonlibrarians. I transfer my list to an Excel® spreadsheet and print it out. When I get to the conference I add the room numbers to the spreadsheet and make any corrections for any sessions that have been canceled or moved to a different room. This is my "bible," and I refer to it many times a day to find out where I should be. I include alternate sessions so that if a session is not what I expect, I know where else I can profitably spend that time.

Be sure you have plenty of business cards. If your organization does not provide them, go to an office supply store and have them made. You really cannot do without them. You need them both for exchanging with colleagues and for entering to win free software, and so on, from exhibitors. (I make it a practice not to enter to win anything I do not really want to have. It's only fair.) You will need them even at conferences that issue cards that exhibitors can scan to capture your information. Not all vendors will have rented scanners.

Pack comfortable clothing and shoes. Appearance really doesn't matter much at these affairs, although you will want to dress more professionally if you are presenting a paper or moderating a session. If you are tired or sore you won't get the most benefit from the conference and might even miss an important session. Plan to dress in layers—one room may be very cold and another a furnace. You should always have a jacket with two pockets. Use one for incoming business cards (from others) and one for outgoing (yours). It is very embarrassing to start to hand someone another person's card. When you receive a person's business card, look at it, then put it in your pocket. (Gentlemen, not in the rear pocket of your pants, please.) After you are out of sight of the person who gave you the card, either jot a note on the back so you will remember why you took the card or, if you just took it to be polite and have no further need of it, throw it away.

During the conference, I suggest the following priorities:

1. *Informal networking with colleagues.* Take every opportunity to speak with other librarians, regardless of the size of their library, geographic location, or subject specialty. We can learn from all. Nowhere else can you talk to as many people as quickly and inexpensively.
2. *Exhibits.* This is your chance to see what's new and to get demonstrations and free searches. Ask if you can have a free password for a period after the conference to explore the product further.
3. *Sessions.* Although the technical presentations are ostensibly the reason you are at the conference, they often go over old ground or, if new, are so crowded that you cannot get into the room. You may want to buy the conference proceedings or tapes of popular or particularly high-rated speakers. Get handouts if you can. *Hint:* If the session is not as advertised or turns out not to be as interesting as you thought it would be, get up and leave. Old conference hands do this all the time, and few speakers will be offended. Often, it is the only way to get to all the sessions you want to hear. Stay focused—remember your objectives.

Use your file folders to keep things straight. One might be for session handouts, one for vendor literature, and so on. You might want to arrange your information by day of the conference. Use a hotel envelope for all your receipts.

The exhibit hall requires its own strategy. On your first visit to the exhibit hall, just look it over and locate vendors you especially want to see. Then, start on one side or the other (from left to right is counter to how most people work, so I do it that way) and systematically make your way through the hall. Do not waste time (yours and theirs) talking to vendors you are not interested in. Say hello, and walk on. If you think you might be interested later or the vendor is new to you, pick up literature only. Even better, just give the exhibitor your business card and ask the person to ship you the literature after the conference. Make sure you go up and down every aisle and exhibit area. When you stop for the day, make a note of where you left off. If there is a vendor you really need to talk with, make an appointment for a later time. The last day is usually slow, and they will have more time to talk with you. This is also a good time to stock up on pens and pencils. The vendor does not really want to pay for return shipping.

At the exhibits, just pick up all the literature that looks interesting. When you get back to your hotel room, go through it all. What looked interesting on the exhibit hall floor may look irrelevant in the room. (I can't tell you how many times I've asked myself, "Why on earth did I pick this up?") If only part of something is worth saving (pages of a catalog or journal), then tear that part out (writing the citation on the pages) and throw away the rest. (Maids must hate library conventions. My wastebasket is always overflowing.) You can ship materials home rather than carrying them, but I find this encourages you to save too much.

When you get home, file what you brought home, going over it once again to make sure you really need it. Immediately write a conference report for your boss or, if he or she does not want one, for yourself. (It is probably a good idea to send at least a short summary of the conference to your boss in any case.) Include any new ideas you got, tips or techniques found, your opinion of any new products (especially of those you want to try), people you met (and why they are important to you), and anything else you want to remember. This last idea sounds obvious, but write down anything you volunteered for. You will be surprised how much you will forget.

File the business cards you kept, and write follow-up letters to people you especially want to thank or stay in contact with. Start planning now for the next conference.

Dealing with People

I find that the most important aspect in time management is making sure that I fully understand each enquiry. It's important to grill the enquirer for as much information as possible about whether some searching has already been done and using what sources, the type and format of data needed and, lastly, what the expected time-frame is, so that other work can be prioritised. Done properly, all this can save so much time and makes the information specialist look very professional and thorough.

British high-tech information specialist

Dealing with people is the most difficult part of a librarian's job. Books and data are easy—they don't have feelings or get angry, depressed, tired, or bored. However, one of the reasons librarians often give for going into this profession is "I like to work with—or help—people." There is nothing better than helping someone find the answer to a pressing problem and being told how much you are appreciated. Now all we have to figure out is how to deal with the rest of our clients.

Koch writes about four kinds of people:

1. Lazy and stupid. They are harmless.
2. Hard working and smart. They take care of the details.
3. Hard working and stupid. They are a menace; fire them or avoid them; create busywork for them.
4. Lazy and smart. They are creative, efficient, and get the most *results*! (Koch, 187, adapted from General Von Manstern writing about the German Office Corps).

I am sure that we all have encountered someone who fits into each of these categories. We librarians tend to fall into group 2. I fit into group 4. I have always said that I am lazy, which is why I am efficient—I do not want to do any more work than I have to.

Schein (1992: 228–253 in Stueart and Moran, 95) says:

Employees are always happier when they can accept the culture of the organization in which they work . . . managers reinforce the organizational culture by (1) what they pay attention to; (2) the way they react to critical incidents and crises; (3) how they allocate rewards; (4) the way they carry out role modeling and coaching; (5) what methods they use for selection, promotion, and removal; and (6) their various organizational rites, ceremonies, and stories.

Goodale (85–86) has some good suggestions for improving morale. Although written for small engineering firms, it reads just as well for small libraries.

First, develop a clear vision for your firm [library] and make certain that senior staff embrace that vision. The firm's president [library's manager] must assume responsibility not only for shaping the vision but also for bringing it to fruition. How does the firm [library] define itself? What do the leaders want the firm [library] to be known for? What is the firm [library] going to look like in five years? How large will it be? Who are the employees likely to be? Which types of clients will it serve? What kinds of opportunities will there be for employees? Every employee should know the answers to these questions.

Second, make firm-wide communication a high priority. Share as much information as possible about the internal workings of the firm [library] to keep staff engaged. Reporting these data to all employees will open communication lines throughout the firm [library], build trust, and fire up the troops.

Third, establish a clear chain of command. A well-delineated hierarchy is especially important for small firms [libraries] because it provides staff with a clear understanding of who reports to whom and how each staff member fits into the general scheme of things. It's important for each member of the staff to have just one supervisor, regardless of whether he or she works on projects overseen by other senior staff members. One of the weaknesses of many small firms [libraries] is that staff members often feel as if they have several supervisors and must meet expectations that are sometimes conflicting. It's important for each employee to have one supervisor and for this supervisor to be available to provide feedback, help, or advice. The firms' [library's] structure should also provide for growth—that is, it should be flexible enough to accommodate staff expansion.

Fourth, demand accountability. Engineers [librarians], for the most part, are such nice people that they hate to confront nonperformers. High performers resent this, and the risk is that these valued staff members will leave. It's important to set high standards and insist that these standards be met by all.

Fifth, delegate wisely, and give all employees a chance to shine. Your staff members want to produce and contribute, so give them the opportunity to do so. Nothing frustrates up-and-comers more than being stifled by senior management. You won't hold on to them long if you don't let them assume some responsibility. Don't be too controlling. Besides, unless you plan on living forever, why would you want to be indispensable to your company [library]? Get your people involved, and give them some challenges they can sink their teeth into.

Communication

*The most effective communicators spend 80 percent of their time lis-
tening and only 20 percent talking.*

Robert W. Bly

*Effective communication occurs when a message is understood by its
sender and transmitted through a medium to one or more receivers
who understand it and are affected by it.*

Sandra Nelson

Real communication is an interactive process. One person sends a
message, and another receives it. When you are the sender, the trick is
to make sure that the message received is the same as the one you
meant to send. When you are the recipient, the trick is to make sure you
are receiving the right message. You must communicate with your
staff, boss, co-workers, and users in the way in which they prefer. You
must find out how the person you are communicating with wants to
receive information.

"The purpose of management communication . . . is to get something accomplished" (White, 1989, 213). Therefore, it is important to
communicate with your boss and upper management in the way they
do. Make sure management is kept informed of your activities. Remember that management does not like surprises or problems. When a
problem arises that you cannot solve yourself, be sure you approach
management properly. Managers do not want problems; they want solutions. Therefore, make it easy for them to solve the problem by offer-
ing several scenarios for a solution.

Some people want all the details; others want only an executive
summary. If you send a long and detailed report to the executive sum-
mary-type person, he or she probably will ignore it. What a waste of
your time! Find out if it is better to report in writing, or if an oral report
in person is sufficient (such as when there may be questions you will
need to answer). Because today most workplaces are multicultural, be
aware of the ways different cultures interpret words, gestures, and personal space. There are many excellent books on this subject (*see* Appendix A).

You communicate with your users. Design marketing materials,
signs, instructions, and handouts so that they communicate their message clearly. Avoid library terms and library jargon, but do use business
terms or the jargon and terminology of your users. If there is any question as to whether something is understandable, test it out on a nonuser
or a family member. If that person does not understand it, make

changes. If you put out confusing materials, you will just have to spend your time answering the same questions you were trying to avoid.

You also receive communications from others. You need to know what information your users need so that you can ensure you are providing it. To do anything else is a waste of time. You find out what your users want and need from you by asking them. Surveys will give you some answers, but you will get better information by talking to people. Do not forget to ask nonusers what information they use and why they do not get it from you.

It is very important that you match the medium to the message; that is, communicate with others by way of the medium that is most conducive to their reading and understanding what you have to say (Table 2.1).

Table 2.1. Match the medium to the message.

Medium	Complex	Important	Permanent Record Required	Confidential	Urgent
Face-to-face	Y	Y	N	Y	Y
Telephone	N	Y	N	Y	Y
Meeting	M	Y	M	N	M
E-mail	N	M	N	N	Y
Individual letter or memo	Y	Y	Y	Y	Y
Video or audio	M	M	Y	N	N
Group letter or memo	M	M	Y	N	M
Policy manual	Y	Y	Y	N	N

Y, yes; N, no; M, maybe.
Adapted from Nelson, 250.

Remember that there are many ways to present data: You can write data out in sentences (a *narrative*) or you can create tables, graphs, and charts.

Be sure that you know what your management expects from you and your library. Does management want you to maintain the status quo, or be on the leading edge of technology and librarianship? Are you supposed to serve the entire organization, or just one area? You find out these things by asking. If you do not get an answer the first time, ask again. Keep asking (in different ways, if necessary) until you are satisfied that you understand exactly what is expected. If you do not understand what is expected, you can waste a lot of time trying different things to no avail.

Most of our clients are nice, but sometimes you must deal with difficult people. We have all encountered someone who just is not responding to us or who may even be obstructionist or downright hostile. Sometimes you can just ignore the person, but what if this difficult person is your boss or an important customer? Do not spend a lot of time moaning and groaning.

When dealing with complaints, listen; do not fight back. Keep your mouth shut. This will help cut the tension, and lets you find out what you need to solve the problem. Probe; ask open-ended questions to get the details. Empathize. Say, for instance, "I understand exactly how you feel." Apologize if necessary. Or, solve the problem. Make sure it does not happen again. If you do not have the authority to do so, find someone who does (Stewart). Find out what the person's issues are and what you can do to fix the problem. If that does not help, try to change the way you deal with the person. I suggest a combination of the last two.

Being polite does not work on everyone. If it doesn't work, try one of Jacob Weisberg's suggestions. Give up and listen—try not to be resentful, or at least don't let it show. Repeat your message, with more emphasis. Rephrase what you said. Let the person talk, but set a limit of "X" amount of time or "X" words. Some of these may also work when dealing with interruptions. If nothing works and dealing with this person on a daily basis is making you miserable, you should consider polishing up your resume and looking for another job. Suffering, complaining, and becoming frustrated should *never* be an option. For whiners, ask the person what they would like done. Make them come up with the solution, not the problem. If you have the authority, give them the responsibility to start to solve the problem. "The worst way to deal with difficult people is to ignore them and suffer in silence" (Stewart).

In written and oral communication, use the correct words. Some of the consequences of poor communication are unclear instructions, wasted meetings, preventable mistakes, or continually rewritten memos and letters. Make sure that what you say is what you mean. Remember that sometimes nonverbal communication is stronger than verbal communication. What you do not say may be more important than what you do say. When you do not understand, ask for clarification. When speaking, ask the listener to restate what you said so that you can make sure you were understood.

In a conversation, eight kinds of communication are actually going on at once (Clark and Clark, 227):

1. What you mean to say.
2. What you actually say.
3. What the other person hears.
4. What the other person thought he or she heard.
5. What the other person means to say.
6. What the other person actually says.
7. What you hear.
8. What you thought you heard.

Be an active participant in conversations. "Listen, Be an active note-taker, be a visual thinker. Enhancing your tool kit of listening and note-taking skills is a great way to get more value at your next conference—but it is only a start. Part two is actually doing something with the ideas you come up with" (Bernacki).

Finally, when you send something to someone, it is a good idea to include a note saying why you sent it, what is important about it, and what action is needed. Be sure to remember to read what your customers read, no matter how busy you are. Even if you do not understand all the technical details, this will tell you what their hot issues are and will familiarize you with the terminology of the field. It also will save you lots of time when looking for information about new developments and trends and industry news.

Working with Your Boss

One of the most important relationships a special librarian has is the one with his or her boss. You can be the best librarian ever, but if your boss is not convinced of your worth you will not last long. There are many things you can do to maintain and improve the boss–librarian relationship.

For some librarians, the boss is not even a librarian. He or she is not likely to be the top official in the company. Your boss also can be someone entirely outside of the organization (such as a mayor or the members of a board of trustees). The boss has many other people to supervise.

The boss may not even set his or her own priorities; your boss's boss may set them, with or without his or her input. The boss is not interested in the library's day-to-day operations or problems, but only cares that the library functions well. Finally, the boss may or may not be a library user.

You must educate your boss, especially if you are establishing a new library for the organization. Even if there has been a library at your institution forever, you will have to let the boss know who you are, your work style, and what you plan to do. Of course, you will have to learn the same about your boss. What are his or her priorities for the library? Is the budget expandable? To whom does your boss report? And what are the priorities of your boss's boss? Does your boss really have power, or is he or she just a supervisor, with the real decision-making authority resting at a higher level? If your boss is just a supervisor, resist the temptation to go over his or her head and right to the decision-maker.

Kevin Kearns advises that you do not have to use psychological tricks to deal with your boss, nor do you have to become friends with him or her. You do not have to change your style completely to get along with your boss, although you may have to make some modifications. Most importantly, you do not have to give in to your boss. Learn to disagree respectfully and constructively. According to Kearns, to manage upward effectively be sure you understand the structure of the organization. Develop a realistic set of expectations regarding what you want from your boss. Look at your boss's style, strengths, and weaknesses; see how they compare with your own. "Understand that managing upward is not about managing the boss; it is about managing yourself within a complex set of peer and hierarchical relationships."

If you have more than one boss, make sure you know the priorities of each boss and his or her priorities for you. Make each aware of critical deadlines of the other and any potential (or actual) conflicts. When there is a conflict that you cannot resolve, let them work it out, based on a set of alternatives you develop.

What if your boss is "unreasonable?" First, do a reality check. Is he or she really asking too much, or is this just your perception? Ask your fellow employees and colleagues outside the library how they feel about some of your issues. Does you boss treat everyone the same way? If so, then his or her behavior is not personal. Next, do not waste time complaining. Focus on what is positive about your boss. Even the worst boss has *some* good points. Treat the situation as a learning experience—one that can push you to new levels of competence. "If you can work with a nasty boss for a four- or six-month period or longer before leaving for good, do so. You might actually be strengthening your capabilities to work with a wide variety of people—including difficult ones—in the future" (Davidson, *The Complete Idiot's Guide*® *to Managing Stress*, 81).

Clark and Clark (235–236) outline five degrees of authority between your boss and you. You should strive to develop a relationship that will work at the highest level. Here they are, from lowest to highest (Clark and Clark):

1. "You wait for the boss to tell you what to do.
2. You ask what to do (your boss still has to tell you).
3. You make suggestions and recommendations (answers, not questions). You're taking solutions, not problems, to your boss.
4. Your plans or priorities are pre-approved. Perhaps you give a weekly report, but you're pretty much on your own here.
5. You and your boss have reached the point where you don't have to bother him or her with anything. You're in complete control of your destiny."

"Ultimately, you'll be treated by your boss in the way you teach your boss to treat you" (Davidson, *The Complete Idiot's Guide® to Managing Your Time*, 94). Here are some additional hints for "training" your boss. "Senior executives become difficult audiences only when you violate their principles of time and information management" (Rae Cook, 20). Respect the pressures that they work under. Don't run in every few minutes with a question—save them up and ask them all at the same time. Better yet, create a good enough relationship with your boss that he or she trusts you to solve most crises yourself.

When you do talk to your boss, be prepared. Be organized and speak concisely and to the point. You may even want to write out what you want to talk about and send it to your boss ahead of time so he or she can prepare. Bring solutions, not problems. Outline alternatives, and use this time to obtain the opinion or gain the approval of your boss. When talking to senior management, show how you and your library can help them get things done, especially things that are not getting done now. Remember that your boss may have many other responsibilities besides the library. Know how the organization works and how you and the library fit into it. Show him or her, quickly, how what you are presenting will affect the organization. Know the consequences of change, and—especially—know the dollar implications. How do you find out? Consult other managers.

Interpersonal Networking

It is impossible to underestimate the importance, for all librarians, of networking. Often, consulting a source outside your library or asking another librarian is the fastest way to answer a question. If you network, you already have a list of places to go when stumped. In addition, networking is one of our best ways of keeping up with what is going on in the profession.

You can network in many ways. I have already talked about the value of attending national conferences. Local meetings of branches of national library associations are not only more frequent and less expensive, they also can be very rewarding. Take advantage of every opportunity. Talk to everyone. Find out what's new in their libraries and in what ways they might be willing to share resources. Look out for continuing education opportunities sponsored by universities, professional associations, and vendors. (The last are especially useful. They are inexpensive—often free—and you can frequently get free search time or products.)

Networking can also be done in more informal ways. Visit other libraries in your area and introduce yourself. You are much more likely to successfully ask a "friend" for a favor than someone you have never met. You may also want to explore nonlibrary resources in the area, for example, trade associations.. Be sure not to abuse your sources, be willing to reciprocate, and remember to thank them profusely. Remember, as Quint (4) has said, "Libraries do not cooperate, librarians do."

Interruptions

I think the most important thing about managing interruptions is accepting them. I tell people my job description is 'Interruptions.' It's all in your attitude.

A corporate librarian

Julie Nutty gives the definition of an interruption as "an unscheduled event." Davidson (*The Complete Idiot's Guide® to Managing Stress*, 96) says, "Disruption happens. It is the interruption of your routine and the resultant newly imposed activities that bother you." It is critical to remember that if no one interrupted us with questions, we would not have jobs. However, interruptions can be one of the most time-robbing parts of a librarian's day. It is important to know how to handle them effectively. "Don't expect to have a major block of time when you can [work on a big project]. Major blocks of time are very rare!" (Eisenberg, 219). You will have to make them. "Managers who establish one quiet hour during the day are able to do three hours' work in that time" (John Koontz, Associate Professor, Purdue University, Department of Building Construction Management, in Miodonski, 49). Block out a time each day when you can be undisturbed. Arrange for someone to screen your telephone calls. Go somewhere other than the library, if necessary.

An independent information broker says, "Working at home is challenging. The worst interruptions, however, I find are unwanted telephone calls. I'm learning to say no and hang up." A corporate librarian says, "I don't consider customers' usage of the library as interruptions, as being available to them is a large part of my job. But it can be hard to concentrate on a dedicated project. I have turned to using off-peak hours for that kind of project." A British librarian in a not-for-profit organization says:

> My main problem is the fact that our office/work space is in the same room as the collection . . . which means I am constantly interrupted. I find the interruptions leave little time for collection development, cataloging, classification, browsing new titles, etc. I never have any "thinking" time! [People often ignore her assistant and come directly to her, even when she obviously is busy.] I do say, "No, that's not really part of my job" and also explain that I have other deadlines and other customers to deal with. Asking people for realistic targets helps and saying "I can't do it now but I can get it to you in X days' time" helps, but these are only "buffering" measures and may damage the reputation of "helpfulness" I have managed to re-establish. Someone described librarians as the "pathologically helpful" type of person, which totally sums me up!

In an *Industrial Engineer* magazine study, managers reported that the average interruption lasts six to nine minutes. The average recovery time was three to 23 minutes. Managers also said that interruptions were the most stressful part of their work (Davidson, *10 Minute Guide . . .* , 90). Stanley Smith (31) divides interruptions into three categories:

1. *Unnecessary:* avoid these, or terminate them quickly.
2. *Necessary:* handle these at once.
3. *Untimely:* these are necessary but come at inconvenient or inappropriate times. Reschedule them.

The first step in controlling interruptions is to analyze them. How often are you interrupted? By whom? For what reason? For how long? There is a sample form in Appendix B that you can use. You will probably find that the 80/20 rule applies to interruptions as well. Identify the 20 percent who are causing the 80 percent, and develop a way to deal with them.

Now that you know what the problems are, what can you do about them? One of the best ways to avoid interruptions is to anticipate them. Have a plan to deal with each type.

Drop-In Visitors

If the drop-in is an outside person, such as a vendor, make it a library policy not to see such people. If a salesperson drops by, instruct your staff or the organization's receptionist to take a business card and some literature and tell the vendor that you will contact him or her if you need the company's services or more information. Do the same for telephone solicitations. I just say, "I never respond to telephone calls. Send me something in writing." Then I hang up.

Head off drop-in visits by your staff by having regular staff meetings where most questions can be answered. "The main reason people cause an interruption is so they won't forget!" (www.123sortit.com, Interruptions). So, if you meet regularly with your staff, even for as few as ten minutes a day, you can cut down on their need to interrupt you. Also, if your staff members have more than one task to do, they are less likely to interrupt you since if they get stuck on one project they can turn to something else until you are free. You should be able to assign most questions to one of four categories:

1. Questions already answered in print somewhere in the organization: Don't bother me with these.
2. Questions that can be easily answered by a co-worker: Don't bother me with these.
3. Questions that just need a yes or no answer. Ask the question, but make it quick.
4. Questions requiring a supervisor's input. You have to and should want to answer these. Make the time. ("The supervisor has to and wants to answer them." [Davidson, . . . *Managing Stress*, 97].)

"The original intent of an open door policy meant those in management were 'open to hearing' what employees have to say. It was never meant to mean people had *carte blanche* to interrupt you at any and all times of the day" (www.123sortit.com, Interruptions). When someone does interrupt, ask them right off what they want. For example, ask, "What can I do for you?" Another successful method is to arrange your office so you do not sit facing the door. If someone knocks, stand and go to talk with him or her in the hall (or at the door). If they ask, "Are you busy?" say yes. Deal with the issue only if it can be done quickly or if it is a *true* emergency. Postpone, that is, arrange another time to talk. You can also refer visitors to someone else or encourage them to solve the issue themselves. Limit your time with people who have no respect for your time or are always interrupting. "Remember, [unproductive] behavior rewarded is behavior repeated" (Weeks, 56).

You may need to do something more drastic, such as closing your doors (or, if you don't have one, making a barrier of masking tape across the entrance of your cubicle, or a sign). The ultimate answer is to leave your office. Work at home, or find a place within the library or the building where you can "hide." (There is always a place where no one would look for you.) Jacob Weisberg offers this scenario for sending people away without insulting them. Start on a personal note, using their name. Say something nice about them, such as "I'm glad to see you," or "I appreciate your input." Explain that you are busy working on deadline. Make an appointment for later, tell them when to come back, or tell them when you will be available.

You may also interrupt yourself. Do not walk to the copier or fax machine every time you have something to copy or fax; accumulate several items and do them at the same time. Do not use the mail, an e-mail message, the phone, or other people as excuses for interrupting yourself. Group appointments so that all the interruptions are together and you have more blocks of time to work. "'This will just take a minute' usually means at least fifteen minutes. Give the one minute and make an appointment for the other fourteen" (Aslett, 19). Do you wear a pager? Develop the self-control to ignore it when you do not want to be disturbed. I especially like this quote from Davidson (*10 Minute Guide . . .* , 144): "Those who voluntarily—or, for that matter, involuntarily—wear a beeper essentially are giving the message to all others that it's okay to interrupt whatever is going on with them." The same goes for cell phones and that beep that says "You've got mail." If you often forget to tell someone something, make a folder or page in a notebook with the name of each of the people with whom you often deal. When you think of something you need to discuss with them, write it down (or put the paper in the file). When you see them you can take care of several items at the same time (Winston, 43).

Telephone Interruptions

"A telephone call is almost always an interruption" (Weeks, 53). An anonymous sage said, "The reason the computer can do work faster than a human is that it doesn't have to answer the phone" (Silber, 149). In 1997, *The Wall Street Journal* estimated that the average employee received 31 telephone calls per day. The number is probably higher now.

Also, remember that just because the telephone rings does not mean you must answer it. It is there for your convenience, not that of the caller. A "telephone call's urgency is no guarantee of importance" (Cochran, 23).

Put a message on your answering machine or voice mail saying something such as, "I am not answering calls from 9 to 10 [or my assistant is screening my calls] so I can use this time for strategic planning on your account as well as those of others. Please leave a message and I will call you after 10" (adapted from Mackenzie, 67). If you do this on a regular basis—such as the first two hours of the day, people will avoid calling you during this time. However, you absolutely must return all calls received when you are not answering the phone. Doing so will encourage people to leave messages because they are confident you will call back.

When you are answering your phone, ask yourself: "Do I have to take this call *now*? Do I have to talk so *long*?" If you take the call, you are acknowledging that the call or caller is more important than what you were doing at that moment. But is it really? Log your telephone calls—in and out—for a week. Does the 80/20 rule apply?

Schedule a regular telephone hour when you make and return calls. Tell people when this time will be. If you do not want to spend a lot of time on a call, make it just before lunch or just before quitting time. People are in a hurry to leave and will spend less time on the phone. "When your calls are returned, note the time the call was placed. In the future, that is usually the best time to reach that caller" (Pollar, 83). Write that time in your address book or planner next to the person's name.

"A planned telephone call takes less time than an unplanned call" (www.123sortit.com, Voice mail). Prepare a script for an important telephone call so that you do not forget anything and you do not get off track. It will give you more confidence, which will, in turn, come through in the conversation.

Here are some more telephone hints. Keep calls short. Get to the point quickly. If it is an incoming call say, "Hello. What can I do for you?" Tell the caller, "I've just got a minute." Have a telephone memo sheet—those pink "While You Were Out" ones are great—and use it for *all* calls. It reminds you to get all the information (name, from where, day, time, telephone number, and subject). Group important, or like, calls. You will need to get out the information only once. Do not play telephone tag. Leave complete messages, including why you are calling, and what the callee needs to do or provide you, and when they can reach you (Mackenzie).

Fire-fighting or Management by Crisis

Crises or emergencies, whether real or imagined, are some of the worst time wasters. It is important to know the difference between fires and crises, time management problems, and interruptions. Fires include threats to job security, the library, personal security, or user security. Time management problems are mail, work overload, deadlines, meetings, equipment maintenance, personnel issues, book orders, budgets, and cataloging. Interruptions involve trivial details needing immediate responses, visitors, the phone, broken equipment, immediate information needs, reference questions, and salespeople. I have dealt with the last two earlier. Now, what can you do about crises?

Do not over-react. Do not get caught up in the sense of panic and anxiety. Stay calm. Do not reward fire-fighting behavior, and do not let your boss or staff do so. Do not shoot the messenger, just deal with the issue. Assume that crises are going to happen, despite your best efforts to avoid them by planning. Allow some extra time in your schedule for dealing with them. (If they do not materialize, you can always use the time for some other task.) Do not adopt other people's problems.

Nevertheless, some interruptions are necessary. "A librarian's job is to deal with a near constant influx of information, material, and demands for assistance, and interruptions come with the territory. Accepting the reality in which a library operates in [is] one important means of coping with interruptions" (Cochran, 52). You know that you are going to be interrupted a lot. How do you cope? Concentrate fully and completely on each person or activity as you deal with it. Then go on to the next one. "When you focus on what you're trying to accomplish, disruptions simply lose their impact on your productivity. It's only when you let your focus shift to the cause of the disruption that you'll find your productivity slipping" (Davidson, . . . *Managing Stress*, 106).

"Visiting with coworkers is not unimportant [for librarians]. Building and maintaining morale [including your own] among library staff members is very important" (Cochran, 26). But don't overdo it. Excess socializing is a great time waster. Why do you do it? Perhaps you are lonely. If you are stuck in a cubicle or an office all day, with no one but your computer to talk to, wouldn't you be tempted to stop and visit with real live people? The same is true for boredom. Maybe your office is located in the wrong place—near the water cooler or rest room—and people are too tempted to stop and visit when they are lonely or bored. Librarians are always eager to know what's going on—in fact, it is critical to our success. However, too much curiosity can waste our time and that of others. Finally, socializing is frequently used as an excuse to avoid work.

"If you see someone is busily working, always ask, 'Is this a good time for you?' Never assume they are available just because you are." (www.123sortit.com, Interruptions). Practice the Golden Rule of Interruptions: Don't interrupt others, either. Instead of interrupting someone, give him or her a note, folded so it takes a while to open. The note should read: "I can see that you're busy. I need to talk to you. Call me when you're free." Put the note on the person's desk—then leave. Or, you could just send an e-mail.

A Chicago solo librarian gives a good tip:

> If interrupted, don't fight it. I have found that after an interruption it's best to turn to work on the first thing that comes to mind. About five to ten minutes later, my mind gets back to what I was doing by itself and I can switch back almost effortlessly. In the meantime, I got ten minutes of something else done that was probably bothering me but I had suppressed [it]. Knowing that my mind is probably working in the background during the interruption allows me to not resent the person doing the interruption. Often, I find I am more focused after a short pause and the ideas flow more clearly.

Meetings

Avoid meetings with time-wasting morons.

Title of one of Scott Adams's Dilbert cartoon collections

Ferner (175) says, "A meeting brings together a group of people with a common interest and with relevant knowledge and expertise, to accomplish some purpose or goal through a process of group interaction." "In America it is estimated that over eleven million meetings are held each day. Many are too long and many are not even necessary" (Stanley Smith, 37). "Most managers spend up to 10 hours a week in meetings, and 90% say more than half that time is wasted" (Koontz in Miodonski, 49). Take a pencil and paper and add up the cost of a meeting: salaries, benefits, and overhead. Then double it. Don't forget to include the opportunity cost—what everyone *could* have been accomplishing if they had not been in a meeting. Now, is the meeting still worthwhile?

Why do we have so many meetings? LeBoeuf (128–130) suggests that we fail to recognize the cost, we want to provide an audience for someone, to socialize, to escape from being effective, because it has always been done that way, to pass the buck, or to fool people into believing they are participating in important decisions. To the above I add to avoid making a decision or to spread the blame if things go wrong.

Seriously, there are three main types of meetings: information giving, decision-making, and regular (one that is scheduled for the same time every week, month, or year). No matter what the purpose, always ask—is this meeting *really* necessary? Can we accomplish the purpose in another way? Always have a specific purpose or goal. If there is no reason to meet, don't meet. Mackenzie (137) lists various reasons for holding a meeting. I have added alternatives for achieving the same results without a meeting.

1. To coordinate action. Use e-mail.
2. To exchange information. Use e-mail.
3. To motivate a team. You really need to meet.
4. To discuss problems on a regular basis. A meeting is necessary.
5. To make a decision. You can either meet or use e-mail.

If you do not have time to go to a meeting, go to just the part that requires your presence or gives you something of value. Ask if you can send a written report instead or send another person instead. Say that your boss said you should not go (but make sure he or she knows you are using this excuse). Do not be afraid to leave a meeting if all that you needed, or were needed for, is over. Say you have another appointment, rather than staying to be polite. Never attend a meeting unless there is a set working agenda and a set ending time.

Before calling a meeting yourself, ask if the problem can be solved or decision reached without a meeting? "Hold a meeting [only] because it is needed, not because it is Tuesday" (Pollar, 90). Phrase the call for a meeting in terms of the action to be taken: to plan, to decide, to evaluate, to solve—and state the problem (Ferner, 177). For every item on the agenda, add the objective or desired outcome. For example: Discuss budget. Objective: reduce by 10%. To keep a meeting on track, have a white board and write each point on the agenda, whose responsibility it is, and what action is required. Get the group to agree on this. Then follow up with a memo afterward. Put the most important items on the agenda first to make sure they are covered.

Have as few people as possible at the meeting. The length of a meeting is usually closely correlated with the number of people attending. Invite only those with the right skills, who need to be there, and can work well together. If someone important cannot be there, either get his or her input or postpone the meeting. If, during the meeting, a decision cannot be reached because someone is not present, call the person and have him or her join you, either in person or by way of the computer.

Prepare. Is the time and place convenient for all? What length of meeting is appropriate? Is anything special needed? (audiovisuals, documents, or food). Try your best to avoid food at meetings. It will only slow them down. (If you must have food, save it for after the meeting—that will speed things up.) Develop a detailed written agenda, and distribute it to all participants before the meeting. Set time limits for each item on the agenda. Keep track of the time, and remind participants of the amount of time left—and do not extend the ending time. Do not plan too much for one meeting; have two meetings instead. Make sure the meeting takes place at the right time in the process; it should not be too soon (before information is available) or too late (to make a difference). Decide who will lead the meeting. Avoid personality clashes. Keep the meeting focused on business, not social chitchat. Guide the group decision process, keeping people on track, limiting discussion, and trying for consensus rather than a vote.

Consider having the meeting in your office. Have someone hold your calls until you want to be disturbed. As long as the meeting is going well, ignore the telephone and visitors. When the meeting has gone on long enough, start answering the telephone. If people giving reports or even just talking tend to get long-winded, have the person who is talking stand. Most will keep it short, because people generally prefer to sit.

Aslett (27) suggests that you schedule meetings for the morning. This forces you to prepare the day before, morning sessions tend to be shorter, and the rest of the day is free; however, this may waste your most productive time. Some people say not to schedule a meeting around lunchtime or at the end of the day, but Jasper says that if a meeting is at 11 a.m. or 4 p.m., people will be motivated to stay on track and get finished on time. The worst time for meetings is just after lunch. It is very hard to keep people on track when they have full stomachs. To improve punctuality, set the meeting at an odd time—say, 8:20, not 8:00.

Follow-up on meetings. Evaluate how the meeting went, what decisions were made, what action needs to be taken. Was the meeting worthwhile? Did the benefits exceed the costs, that is, the time spent of those who attended. Send out a post-meeting memo with action items for each participant.

Manage Your Absences

If you want to see people panic, remove a sole staffer (from any department) and watch as other employees try to figure out how to get the services that person usually provides now that they're gone.

Anne C. Tomlin

You cannot always be in your library. You have to plan for each type of absence: temporary, short-term, and long-term. Temporary absences are those that take a few minutes, such as delivering a document, getting the mail, buying a cup of coffee, and going to the bathroom. Put a sign on your door or desk that says: "The librarian will be right back. Please wait, or leave a message." (Make sure you leave paper and pencils nearby.)

You might also be away for a day or two during a short-term absence because of such things as an illness, a vacation, off-site training, or jury duty. If you know about the absence in advance, let people know with a sign or by e-mail. (It does not necessarily mean they will plan ahead, but at least they know you will be out.) Arrange to have your mail taken care of, and be sure to leave an appropriate message on your answering machine or voice mail (or have the telephone calls sent to someone else to answer). It is a good idea to have a place for people to leave books and journals, requests for materials, and other things for you outside your door. Make sure it is a secured box so people cannot take items out of it as well.

For longer absences, such as those required by an illness, injury, pregnancy, or a family emergency, you may need to find someone to substitute for you. In some locales, there are library temporary help firms that can find a person to fill in. You could also hire an out-of-work librarian or a recent library school graduate. (I had two of these positions. They were good opportunities for me to see if I wanted to work in that type of library. One even wanted to hire me full-time.) If no one is available, a secretary or clerk may have to fill in. Resist the temptation to let them ask another special librarian to cover for you. He or she already has enough to do handling requests from his or her own library.

Tomlin (20–21) makes an amusing and true point:

> Without a smooth transition to emergency coverage, you will either return to chaos that will take months to repair, or possibly have no job to which to return. The powers-that-be may see your enforced absence as an opportunity to save money by eliminating your salaried position and outsourcing what they consider necessary. Who needs books? They're outdated before they roll off the presses. Journals cost too much; we'll sign up for a document delivery system. Put in a couple more computers and let the docs do their own searching. After all, everything's on the Internet (somewhere) and it's free and full text, right? Aaughh!!!

In any case, you should have a written manual of policies and procedures. This should be supplemented with the names of document delivery services, online searchers, and other consultants that can be called on for services the fill-in person cannot handle. This will help ensure that your clients will get good service. There is also an additional benefit. Your clients will find out the real cost of obtaining information and then will better appreciate the services you provide. Prominently post "how-to" instructions. List Web sites that they may need to consult. If you will be gone a long time, notify vendors to expect delays in processing invoices if they send them during your absence. You may want to suggest they send invoices early, unless they prefer to put the bills—and payments—on hold (guess which they'll choose). Secure sensitive files and other paper and electronic data, such as circulation records, computer passwords or access codes, and original copies of software or videos. Don't forget to set your e-mail to no-mail for the duration, unless you can read it from home. Last, let your customers know that you will be gone as far in advance as possible.

Some Final People-Related Time Management Tips

- Never waste employees' time—do not assign busy work just because they do not look busy.
- Make sure their time savers really are saving their time.
- Separate the important from the merely urgent for them.
- Tell them the why behind a task.
- Give them enough time to get the job done.
- Encourage them to give a task (or customer or telephone call) their full attention.
- Cut down on their time spent in meetings.
- Make sure you provide complete directions the first time, without too many details. These should be in writing so they do not have to call or ask you in person.
- Do not interrupt one project with another unless it is absolutely necessary.
- Do not ask several of them the same questions or assign several the same project. (The president of one company I worked for did this all the time. When they all came to me for help, I would lead them to each other and suggest they work together.)
- Remember to praise and thank people. "People above you know that, when a group does well, it's because someone exhibited leadership. If you take time to praise the group, you stand out as the likely leader of it. It also indicates your ability to facilitate good work" (Davidson, . . . *Managing Stress*, 51).

- Even though this sounds outrageous, there is some truth to Dilbert's Dinosaur Strategy. "ignore all new management directives while lumbering along doing things the same way you've always done them. If you wait long enough, any bad idea will become extinct" (Adams, 128–129).
- Volunteers need to be recognized and appreciated. They are self-motivated or they wouldn't be there. Assign them tasks in line with their abilities and interests. They will only work well at what they enjoy—make sure they do not feel "used." Beware those who think they know something about libraries and try to reorganize things. Set ground rules at the first visit. Use tact when correcting them.
- If you are in an open or shared office or a cubicle, try earplugs when you need to concentrate (or sound-canceling headphones).
- If a vendor seems to have gotten too busy to give you the service you want, find another—perhaps smaller and hungrier—vendor who can. Don't forget to tell both vendors why you switched. Also, try to find vendors that deliver or ship for free.
- "Simplifying your work is important. Simplifying everyone's work is even more so" (Pollar, 152).
- "The best relationships are built on five attributes: mutual enjoyment of each other's company [You won't work well with someone you dislike], respect, shared experience, reciprocity, and trust" (Koch, 181).
- "Most managers spend much more time dealing with subordinates' problems than they even faintly realize" (Oncken and Wass, 179).
- "In general, the people who have helped you the most in the past will also be the people who can do so in the future" (Koch, 181).
- Stay out of petty, partisan office politics, but know what's going on, who's doing what.
- Find out how to get a check (or purchase order) written quickly. It *always* can be done. But don't abuse this privilege.
- Befriending the receptionist, mailroom personnel, president's secretary, and accounting person in charge of your accounts will pay off handsomely.
- "Spend as little time as possible doing things for people they can do for themselves. This can be tricky. Naturally, you don't teach the president how to search the Internet. But many employees want to learn how to find information themselves. The links you share through your Intranet and personal e-mails help you inform your workforce. For those willing and interested to learn, take time to teach them, a little at a time, how to use your Intranet page and what you've made available to them electronically. In the long run, this saves you time. You also develop a personal relationship with

people. They will then often share information discoveries with you" (a corporate librarian).

Dealing with Space

If you spend 20 minutes a day looking for things, that's nearly 12 days per year—or more than most employees' annual vacations. Therefore, it is a good time management technique to arrange your office or desk to increase efficiency. Put what you use most often close at hand. Keep your office and desk neat. Have a place for everything, and put everything in its place. (Yes, this is easier said than done, but it is certainly a goal to strive toward). If you get in the habit of putting things back where they belong when you are finished using them, or doing something to move them off your desk, you will waste much less time looking for things.

Why don't things stay where they belong? According to Tullier (120), there are four main reasons: where they belong is too crowded, things are not arranged well, they do not have a place to belong, or they have a place but are not put there. If you work in more than one place, have duplicate tools and files. It will save you the time involved in moving them from one place to another. At the end of each week, "clean your slate." Transfer all notes to a master list, catch up on phone calls, get rid of clutter, process all remaining mail, make next week's to-do list, and put out what you will be working on first on Monday (Aslett, 4).

Is the saying, "A clean desk is a sign of a cluttered mind" true? No. A clean desk is a sign of a clean desk—nothing more. It could mean that you have hidden everything. A messy desk may not be a sign of disorganization, just a sign of a different kind of organization, especially in a creative, right-brained person. "For some people, clutter sends a message of junk and unfinished business. For others of us it is like an old and trusted friend who comforts us" (McGee-Cooper, 75). Make sure you are comfortable with the message your desk sends. If your boss is a clean-desk person, a messy desk may tell him or her that you are disorganized. On the other hand, a messy-desk boss may see your clean desk as a sign that you do not have enough to do.

Use your desk only for work. "Develop the habit of using a certain spot exclusively for work-related activities and you will find it much easier to automatically settle down to the job at hand when it is time to do so" (Nauman, 57). Identify the active areas in your workspace (usually the closest or most convenient), and keep them free of clutter. Clutter costs *time*: to store it, to dig through it to find something, and to clean it or around it. Do not be a pack rat. "Clutter is the enemy of efficiency" (Bly, 128). Clutter or disorganization will not simply get better by itself. You and no one else must do something about it. And, it will come back if you do not change your ways.

Why can't you get rid of clutter? According to Tullier (94), you may feel guilty because you spent so much money on an object, or you may think that you should save it because someday it may be worth something. We also keep things for sentimental reasons or because we feel it has "historical" value (either personally or organizationally). Some of us are pack rats, too thrifty (or cheap) to throw anything away. Comedian George Carlin does a great routine on "stuff"—we must have a place for our stuff. We may even feel our stuff is part of our identity.

To get rid of clutter, look at all of it and sort it into in four piles: junk to be dumped, things to be filed, things you can pass on to someone else, and items that need more thought. Then go through the piles and winnow those down, too. If you are really disorganized and buried under paper, you may have to go in on a weekend. Tackle your desk first, starting with the top, then the drawers. Go on to other theoretically "visible" surfaces (which may actually be buried). Do the files last (Winston, 59–60). "Sometimes, instead of your desk, it makes sense to start [organizing] with storage areas such as cabinets, closets, and bookcases. By organizing storage areas, you free up space to house material from the areas you subsequently organized" (Haddock, 59).

Turner uses the acronym SPACE to help you remember the five steps in organizing your office. "SPACE stands for Sort, Purge, Assign a home, Containerize, and Equalize." First, sort. Ask yourself, "Do I really need this?" Where should it be housed? "You'll get the most visual bang for your buck by sorting the things you can see first. The things that are out, in sight (and in the way?) are probably being used more than what's squirreled away. Group like items together." Then, purge. "Purge doesn't necessarily mean to throw something away. Purging an item from your space is an invitation (or an order!) for that item to move elsewhere." The next step is to assign everything a home. "Storage is about being able to take your things out again with the greatest of ease. If you can't find something, can't reach it, or can't use it because it was improperly stored, what good is it anyway? Keep things and information where they will be used. Active and heavily used reference files are best kept in file drawers at your fingertips. A smaller number of files can be readily seen and accessed from a stepped file holder. Diskettes scattered about could be given one home in a bin next to your computer." The fourth step is to containerize. "Use containers to hold like items together and keep things within fixed limits. The finite space of a container also makes it difficult for you to collect much more than your container will allow itself to hold." Finally, equalize or maintain your system. Most people think this step is boring and avoid it, but a system not maintained is a system that doesn't work (and the time you spent organizing is wasted). "The idea is not to take too long. Do what needs to be done and get back in the race. Set aside time every day for equalizing."

You might not want to use a desk at all. A corporate librarian wrote, "I read an article in *Business Week* about a CEO who does not sit at a normal desk, because it slows him down. He finds it [standing up] much more efficient. I have tried it when I need to organize my desk after a hectic period and it works for me, too. I'm much more efficient standing than sitting behind my desk."

Do you like your space? Is it *you*? If not, ask yourself what you can do about it. You can always do something. To brighten up your work environment, perhaps you can add a plant; an extra lamp; or photographs of your family, pet, or favorite vacation spot. If possible, eliminate distractions, such as noise, poor lighting, or the wrong temperature. To gain more storage, try a lazy Susan, undershelf baskets or shelves, corner cabinets, toolboxes, or tackle boxes. "If you use it daily, it can live on top of your desk. If you use it weekly, it can live inside your desk. If you use it monthly, it can live in your office, if you use it less than monthly, it can be put in off-site storage" (Hemphill, 70). Nowadays your primary work area is likely to be around your computer, not your desk. If so, rearrange things so that what you need is close at hand. Put most of the "stuff" you will use most often in the space between your desk and your computer.

Delegating

Managers must delegate. If you are spending your time doing things others could be doing for you, who will do the things only you can do?

Kathleen R. Allen

QUIZ: Delegation (adapted from Haddock).

1. Do you regularly take work home?
2. Do you regularly work over 48 hours a week?

3. Do you often continue to help subordinates or others once you have given them a task to do?
4. Are you buried with work after a vacation or other time away from work?
5. Do you have no one to relieve you?
6. If you have been promoted recently, are you still doing any of the tasks you did before the promotion?
7. Are you always too busy?
8. Do you always seem in a rush?
9. Do you often do something yourself rather than teaching someone else how to do it?
10. Do you seldom have time for professional education?
11. Are you worried that your job will be eliminated?
12. Do you like to have your fingers in every pie?
13. Are there things you do that almost anyone could do?
14. Do you hesitate to let your staff do things their own way?
15. Do you spend time on details that could better be spent on planning?

If you have answered "yes" to more than five questions, you need to learn how to delegate more effectively.

"To delegate is to achieve specified results by empowering and motivating others to accomplish some of the results for which you are ultimately accountable" (Ferner, 155). It is one of the basic tenets of good management. You should *never* do something that a) someone else could do better or b) could be done by someone making less money. After all, we justify our existence on the basis of doing less expensively what higher-paid people should not be doing. Shouldn't we apply the same principle to our own work? Continually ask yourself, "Do I personally have to do this?" (Clark and Clark, 146). Delegation keeps you focused on what you're best at and what you like to do best. Not delegating is also selfish; it does not let others learn the skills they need to succeed. "Helping junior members of your organization *always* looks good to those above you, especially at performance-review time" (Davidson, . . . *Managing Stress*, 51). You also free yourself by learning to delegate effectively. "Delegation authorizes and entrusts someone other than you to accomplish the tasks at hand" (Turner). Delegate if it will take less time to train someone than doing it yourself. Delegate if you need to train someone to do the job the next time. Yes, you will have to spend some time teaching a beginner; however, there are two benefits. First, the beginner can do the job less expensively than you can. Second, you will be "finding someone who will gain confidence, grow with you, and become a valuable long-term ally" (Turner).

Delegation even goes back to the Old Testament. The father-in-law of Moses, Jethro, told Moses to choose leaders and delegate the day-to-day decision-making to them, freeing him for long-term, high-level thinking (LeBoeuf, 160). If you let someone else do a job for you, "while that task was being done, you were doing something else, thus effectively multiplying your time, which is the ultimate time-management technique" (Allen, 45). According to Cochran (80), special librarians are good at delegating.

Even nonmanagers can delegate. "[Delegating] may sound like an odd suggestion for solos but there's no reason why some library tasks can't be assumed by other departments" (Tomlin, 8). You can delegate laterally ("Can you do me a favor?"), upward ("Boss, can you call so-and-so and get them to give me the information I need to complete my project?"), or downward ("If you want this done, can you lend me your assistant to help?").

Why don't we delegate more often? There are many reasons: It does not occur to us, it seems a sign of weakness, it seems "immoral" not to work hard, the task is enjoyable and we want to do it ourselves, it may go wrong if we are not in control, it takes time to train and supervise someone, it might take longer or be less good if someone else does it, the boss says *I* have to do it, it makes us seem or feel indispensable, we would have to leave our personal comfort level, or we might lose control of the process. Ainsworth (19–20) wrote as an accountant, but these ideas hold for librarians as well:

1. "Clients want *me* to do it." "Your clients will understand when you do not perform every little detail for them on everything. In fact, I found that my clients respected by time more after I began delegating some client contact to staff."
2. "The work I do is too complex to trust to subordinates." "If you have procedures in place for proof and control and have conveyed to subordinates your commitment to quality, then they will do it to the customer's satisfaction."
3. "I do not have any subordinates." "If you want to [do] more, then hire someone."
4. "It takes too long to train someone." Yes, it does take time and sometimes it is very frustrating, but it is worth it. "Learn to delegate. You can save time and be a mentor. With a little training/mentoring, junior staff can handle a lot of [quick reference] requests that take up a lot of your time. They get experience, you get

less interruptions and have more time—everybody benefits" [Canadian business librarian].

5. "I can't find good employees." Use the acronym EARRS: enthusiasm, aptitude, resourcefulness, responsibility, and skills.

Once you decide to delegate, make sure you do it right! Here are some guidelines:

- Select the right person (or firm). Who can do the job? (Who has the skills, time, interest?)
- Provide the necessary resources. If additional resources (money, people) are needed, where can they come from (outside, other departments, other people)?
- Determine what training is available to help this person (or someone else). What will be the effect of adding this task to this person's current duties, to their morale? Which of this person's current duties can be eliminated, streamlined, or reassigned?
- Delegate both the good and the bad (not just the dirty work). "Give the task importance." Don't downgrade it; you may get poor results (Griessman, 141).
- Take your time. Allow subordinates time to learn.
- Delegate gradually. Do not transfer authority overnight.
- Delegate in advance. Do not wait until the last minute.
- Delegate the whole. Do not divide a job. Assign both responsibility and authority, then hold the person responsible for the outcome. "Delegation without authority is empty. Before delegating think carefully whether you are willing to permit work to be done without your direct oversight or review. Too much review, especially of professionals, breeds apathy, dependency, and passive resistance, and destroys motivation" (Veaner, 129, in Stueart and Moran, 111).
- Delegate for specific results. Describe the results, not the steps. Avoid gaps and overlaps.
- Consult before you delegate. Let subordinates have a say in what they get to do. Delegation gives the employee the why, and assignment gives only the what.
- Leave the subordinate alone. Do not micromanage; let go. Accept someone doing something a way other than the way you would have done it, assuming it accomplishes the task. Accept imperfection (which is not the same as sloppy work). Do not be overly critical; let the person fail somewhat. Be available for questions. Be open to new ideas or ways of working. Reward the person. "The things that get rewarded get done" (LeBoeuf quoted in Bly, 110).

"Set precise objectives, but give only general guidelines for achieving them" (Stanley Smith, 55). Remember, there is more than one right way to do something; encourage creativity.

- Review the project's progress. Do not wait until the end of the project to find out that things are not going well.
- Make sure the delegatee gets the credit.
- Make sure both sides know the scope of the job, the deadlines, authority level (all, some, none), the budget, outcomes expected (report, product). Those above, below, and on the same level must know who is responsible for what—and must agree to it. Keep a list of tasks assigned to others. Review these periodically so you do not let something fall through the cracks. (*See* Appendix B for some forms you can use to keep track of what you delegate.)

Not everything can or should be delegated. If you are a manager, you must retain leadership activities, personnel matters, counseling or morale problems, things your boss asked you to do *personally*, confidential or legal matters, things for which there is *really* no time to explain, and those tasks that are best done by you or can *only* be done by you. Also, you will not want to delegate those professional activities, such as searching, that form the core of your value to your organization.

"Delegating to subordinates is easy. The hard part is delegating to co-workers and your boss. Always appeal to the principle of 'efficiency' when you try to fob off your work sideways or upward" (Adams, 77). To continue in this semiserious mood, "The real 'low-hanging fruit' of work avoidance involves any task that has more importance to somebody else than it has to you. If you ignore this type of task long enough, eventually the person who really needs it done will offer to do it, even if it's clearly your job" (Adams, 78). Good time management requires using common sense. If you do not have time to do something and can delegate it to the original requestor (particularly low-priority or low-profile tasks), so much the better.

If you are a manager, resist upward or reverse delegation. Do not let others bring you their problems. Make sure that if you delegate a task to a subordinate it stays there. Do not take it back, even if the subordinate appears to be failing. Instead, help the person complete the task. If you have chosen the right person, he or she will learn.

How do you choose the delegatee? Ask who can do this best (besides you)? If it is a task you do only occasionally, is there someone who does this all the time and is an expert in this area? (I used this logic for outsourcing original cataloging to the State Library.) Is there someone who can do it less expensively? Is there anyone who can do the job now, whereas I might not have the time? Would this task contribute to the training or development of one of my people?

"Assign tasks to the most junior person who has the skills and rank necessary to complete the assignment successfully. If no one meets these criteria, find or train someone" (Winston, 243). "Find out what people do well and find ways to let them do more of it" (Pollar, 69). *Siess's corollary:* Hire people who have the skills you want, then leave them alone to use them. "Hire people smarter than you, with talents in different areas, and let them shine. Pick people who can accept responsibility. Not everyone can" (Pollar, 82).

"In general, people to whom you delegate should be qualified, willing and accountable" (Messmer, 21). You can train for specific skills. If the job is critical, hire someone already trained. If you have some leeway, take a flier on someone with "potential" who can work hard and is eager to learn.

Finally, here are some other thoughts on delegation from a variety of librarians. A British high-tech corporate librarian says:

> Philosophise rather than plan. In other words, look at the big picture rather than the small one, and measure your daily activities against it. In our case, to be serious for a minute, we reckoned that too much of our time was being used on activities that the end-user didn't need us for. The prime example was managing journal subscriptions—over 300 of them—for departments outside the library. We set up the subs via an agent, received the journals, re-addressed them, dealt with non-arrivals, contacted people about renewals, and so on. My assistant spent 60% of her time doing nothing else. We have now set up a page on our intranet site that allows people to make direct contact with the publishers and set up their own subs online—an instant saving of time that we can now devote to activities that benefit the whole user community and not just a selected few members of it.

An independent information broker says:

> As the owner of a small business, the hardest thing is to give up control and let other people do things. Even though it takes longer to train someone to do something, it pays off in the end. Being stuck in bed for two months [with a broken ankle] forced me to delegate a lot of work I would not normally have given up. My staff is more productive and more knowledgeable because of it.

A corporate librarian says: "Keep up with the routine the best way you know how. It's like the dishes in the sink. The maintenance will always be there for slow days. If the slow day never comes, try to get temp or intern help or set aside the first 20 minutes of your day to hack away at

it." Another says, "Having a part-time library assistant actually compli-
cates things! It's not that I need to fill up his time—he has plenty to do.
It's just that occasionally we duplicate our efforts." A corporate librarian with another point of view says:

> My biggest time manager trick is to hire an intern! Let's face it, you
> can do all the tricks in the world and still not have enough time. Usu-
> ally budgetary constraints are a big problem. Interns often do work
> for credit, but we do pay our interns. There are so many tasks and
> projects that an intern can perform. What's even more beneficial is
> that the interns usually bring fresh perspectives and new ideas to the
> organization. Most beneficial!

Outsourcing

Outsourcing is similar to delegating, but is usually assumed to be hiring
a service, company, or person outside the library to do a specific task,
that is, paying someone else to do a part of your job. Used correctly,
outsourcing can be a big time saver.

When should you outsource? Generally, you should outsource
when it is to your advantage, when you can control it, when it can improve service levels at no extra cost, when a contractor would more
easily be able to stay current with technology, or when you need expertise not available in-house. Caldwell (1996) says, "What we outsource
is not our organization's core business, but it is that of the vendor, who
is in a better position to deliver a quality product." Outsourcing can
also take care of a temporary overload. We all face times when everyone wants something at the same time; outsourcing can help. Finally,
outsourcing can be a good way to offer a new service with minimal
risk. If it does not go over well, you can just drop the outsourcer. You
must decide which of your services are mission-critical and which can
be done only, or best, by you. You can outsource work to another
department within the organization or to another organization. Both
have pros and cons. It might seem safer to outsource internally. There
should be no problem with internal outsourcing, as long as we make
sure there is added value; we are just partnering inside the organization
rather than outside of it.

What should you outsource? What should you *not* outsource? Contract out those tasks you do not do well so that you can concentrate on
what you do best. If you are not a cataloger, contract out cataloging to
give you more time to do the online searching or database building that
you do outstandingly. You can also use outsourcing to add expertise that

you do not have. If you have a project that will require a lot of detailed chemical searching, but you are not a chemist, why not outsource those searches to an expert chemical searcher? The expert will do it better than you could, making your patron happy and, indirectly, making you look good.

The most common library services outsourced are journal subscriptions, document delivery (books and articles), cataloging, and online searching. Using a subscription service does not save money but does save time. It can allow you to handle subscriptions that otherwise would require hiring another employee. You might be able to handle document delivery for your clients, but is it worth your time? What will you have to not do to provide this service? Is locating, retrieving, and perhaps even photocopying articles something that only you can do? Why not pay someone else to locate the items, arrange payment, and ship them to you? Using a book jobber can save you time, money, and aggravation. Let someone else place the orders and deal with short or lost shipments. I calculated that using a jobber gave me 20 percent more free time each day. The most often outsourced job is cataloging. If you like cataloging, are good at it, and have the time, then by all means do it. But find someone else to do it if you don't like it, aren't good at it, or don't have the time. Most librarians feel, and rightly so, that online searching is the most professional and most valuable of their services and that this is the one service they should retain in-house. It should be outsourced only to add value or as a last resort.

Some Final Time Management Hints

Here are some more ideas for saving time, covering different topics.

- Substitute: Use electronic copy instead of hard copy; let vendors manage and store periodicals for you.
- Simplify: KISS (keep it short and simple). Examine every repetitive task you perform to see if you can streamline it.
- "I usually try to do my more involved searches after 5:00 when there are fewer interruptions" [a Chicago solo]—or do them early in the morning when fewer people are online.
- "Some projects I break into sections. This may *seem* to take longer, but actually makes the project more 'interruptible.' I don't lose my place as dramatically and recover the project better after the interruption. This works for me. For example: alphabetizing catalog cards" [another Chicago solo].

3
Dealing with Job Stress

Stress is Nature's Way of Telling You to Let Go!

Jeff Davidson

There's no doubt about it: Work can be, and usually is, stressful.

Richard Carlson

What Is Stress?

Stress is a natural physiological reaction to danger. It is a *necessary* biological function. Without stress and its physical manifestations, humans would not avoid dangerous situations. Meredith says:

> Stress is commonly viewed as a frustrated "fight or flight" response. A basic human survival mechanism left over from our primordial "roots" when we could best respond to perceived dangers by either fighting or fleeing; seen in this way, stress behaviour and emotions are sometimes regarded as problematic inappropriate responses to threatening situations in modern civilised society, however, stress is a) a powerful internal communication to raise awareness, and b) a source of energy, although the raw emotional and physical energies may have to be transformed to a more useful form before they are directly useful.

Nature has thoughtfully provided us with a warning sign—stress. However, too many of us ignore the warning.

There are many sources of stress, but only one will be dealt with in this book—the stress we feel in our jobs, and specifically library job stress. In *The Complete Idiot's Guide® to Managing Stress*, Davidson (20–21) describes four types of stress. *Anticipatory stress* happens when we are concerned about the future or about events that have not yet happened. Much of what we worry about never even happens. The second type of stress is *situational*, the stress of the moment. This is a more reasonable form of stress. We are concerned about what is happening to us right now. *Residual stress* is worry about events that took place in the past. We try to figure out what we could have done differently. (This is also called guilt.) Finally, *chronic stress* is stress that continues over a long period of time. It can come from any of the first three, but is characterized by the fact that it does not seem to go away.

What are some library examples of each kind of job stress?

1. *Anticipatory:* your upcoming performance review, that big project due next week, whether the library will be hit by the next round of downsizing, who will be the next director, the mountain of filing that awaits you, an upcoming presentation or speech, being called into the boss's office, or having to fire an employee.
2. *Situational:* a confrontation with an angry user, an online search that is not finding any relevant hits, difficulty finding an item in your files, a crying employee, a phone call that interrupts your train of thought, a nearby colleague talking loudly on the telephone, or a broken copying machine.
3. *Residual:* the raise you thought that you would get but did not, a presentation that did not go well, losing an employee, or the feeling that if you would just have had more time you could have done a better online search.
4. *Chronic:* being asked to do more with less; a noisy air conditioner fan that never gets fixed; being underpaid and overworked; not getting the respect you expect and deserve from management; employees who do not use the library; hearing, "It's all on the Internet, and it's all free"; or the increasing demands of keeping up with technology, change, and the increasing rate of change.

In addition, there is good stress and bad stress. Shellenbarger says:

Good stress is the kind that motivates and excites, the kind most likely to yield good results on the job. . . . [Also called Challenge stress, it] is linked to having lots of projects, assignments and responsibilities, leading to things employees value—such as money, skills or promotions—and it tends to be reported by employees who are also loyal, satisfied with work and unlikely to be looking for a new job. Bad stress is the kind that fouls performance. Hindrance stress [or bad stress] is linked to red tape, stalled careers, lack of job security, confusion of over job goals and the degree to which politics rather than performance shape employer decisions. [It] tends to be reported by employees who are dissatisfied or looking for another job.

Unfortunately, both kinds of stress impact our ability to work productively and happily.

Often, we are our own worst enemies. As Davidson (. . . *Managing Stress*, 5) puts it, "For most people, most of the time, most of the stress they encounter is self-induced." Not only do we worry about things that have not happened yet, or continue worrying about things that happened hours, days, or even years ago, but we also worry about things that never even happened—about perceived injustices or misinterpreted comments by others. But if we can create our own stress, we can also *un*create it. We can learn how not to worry, not to obsess, not to put ourselves in harm's way.

"A majority of managers say their jobs are more stressful than a decade ago. Many predict that their jobs will become even more stressful in the next three to four years" (Davidson, . . . *Managing Stress*, 110–111). In a Yankelovich Monitor survey of 2,500 workers, 33% reported feeling an increase in stress over the past year (Shellenbarger). This does not need to happen. If we learn how to deal with situations at work we can make our jobs *less* stressful, now and in the future. We do not have to react to these situations in the same old stressful way. We can—and must—stop the stress cycle.

Job stress is a "psychological and physiological reaction that takes place when you perceive and imbalance in the level of demand placed on you and your capacity to meet that demand. In plain English, you're up against something and you're not sure you have what it takes to meet the challenge" (Davidson, . . . *Managing Stress*, 19).

How can you deal with job stress? "The more control employees have over their own work and the more information they have about possible changes that will occur, the less likely they are to feel job-related stress" (Stueart and Moran, 205). Tell your boss you're overcommitted, overworked, or in over your head. Be proactive, decide that you are more important that your work and just say no—to overtime, to a promotion, to increased travel, or to whatever is causing us stress. "Despite the promise of more leisure time through advances in technology, particularly in the information industry, spare time seems as elusive as ever for most professionals, including librarians" (Cochran, 4–5).

Where Does Stress Come From?

I Love My Job!
I love my job, I love the pay!
I love it more and more each day.
I love my boss, he is the best!
I love his boss and all the rest.

I love my office and its location, I hate to have to go on vacation.
I love my furniture, drab and grey, and piles of paper that grow each
    day!
I think my job is really swell, there's nothing else I love so well.
I love to work among my peers, I love their leers, and jeers, and
    sneers.
I love my computer and it software; I hug it often though it won't
    care.
I love each program and every file.
I'd love them more if they worked a while.

I'm happy to be here. I am. I am.
I'm the happiest slave of the Firm, I am.
I love this work, I love these chores.
I love the meetings with deadly bores.
I love my job—I'll say it again—I even love those friendly men.
Those friendly men who've come today,
In clean white coats to take me away!!!!!

From The Lost Dr. Seuss Collection,
anonymous, found on the Web

In the previous section we saw that we can be our own worst enemies when it comes to stress. This is particularly true of librarians. "Librarians tend to be some of the most over-committed service professionals" (Cochran, 64). "Many librarians feel challenged, and perhaps a
bit overwhelmed, by the scope of the information profession today"
(Cochran, 12). It used to be fairly easy to keep up with the library and
information world. It used to be fairly easy to meet the information
demands of our users. They would ask for books or magazine articles
and we would supply them either from our own collections or through
the ILL system. Reference questions were answered from our own
knowledge or our collection. And, for the most part, that was it.

Now there are new sources to consult: online databases, online
journals, and, of course, the Internet and the World Wide Web. Days
for delivery of books or journals from the ILL system or other vendors
are no longer acceptable to our users. At the same time as we are being
asked to deliver more information from more sources in shorter times,

the questions that our customers are asking are more sophisticated, more complicated, and more difficult to answer. This all leads to an increased level of stress for librarians.

Another source of stress on information workers is the long-standing frustration of not being able to keep up with the workload. Cochran says:

> To some degree, the frustration that librarians may experience about not finishing a task may be a matter of perception. Too often, it seems that librarians focus on tasks they have *not* accomplished—books remaining to be cataloged, reference questions to be answered, and looseleaf service releases to be filed—rather than on those they *have* completed [emphasis mine]. In even the smallest of libraries, the work never seems to be completely done. Rarely able to be able to celebrate closure of one project before moving to the next, many librarians feel that they spend most of their days running to keep up rather than running to stay ahead.

In addition, due to cutbacks in staff and resources, libraries often are asked to continue to serve their clients at the same level—or even to increase services. How could librarians *not* feel stressed in these circumstances? Other causes are the ever-increasing rate of change, organizational change, role conflict, and downsizing.

A major issue is information overload. Berkman (6) defines information overload as follows:

> . . . the feeling of frustration and/or anxiety we get when we perceive and inability to attend to the information that we believe we should be attending to. [It occurs] when a person's capacity for processing information is exceeded and interferes with making decisions; when information received becomes a hindrance rather than a help; having too many varied types of data inputs and channels which add to rather than replace existing ones; when it's impossible to stay current.

He divides information into four categories:

1. *Aggressive:* demanding, impatient; "You MUST attend to me now!" E-mail, telemarketing, advertising, phone calls.
2. *Passive-aggressive:* guilt-inducing; "You SHOULD be attending to me." Newspapers, newswires, professional reading, voice mail, media, walk-in visitors.
3. *Friendly:* quietly waiting; "I'm here if you need me." Books, government sites, television and radio news, reference materials, bookmarks.

4. *Customized:* information that does not yet exist, comes into being from your queries. Interviews, questions, workshops, results of online searches, narrowly focused alert services.

To cope with information overload, Berkman (6) suggests, the following: "Examine your feelings; can you change how you think? Understand that just because a message or piece of information seems to be demanding your attention, it does not automatically mean you must attend to it and respond immediately. Differentiate between urgent and important. Don't sacrifice the important for the urgent. Accept that you can't keep up."

According to Davidson (. . . *Managing Stress*, 46), the number one stressor in the workplace is competition and "your 'most challenging competitor' is you." We—or our employers—create unrealistic expectations of what we should be able to accomplish. Our colleagues, often in larger, better-funded libraries, are writing and speaking at professional conferences about the wonders they are performing. Due to improvements in professional communication, we can easily learn of these services and feel that we must provide the same to our clients— even if we have neither the time nor resources to do so, or even if we have not been asked to do so. In attempting to do too much, we may make "impossible" service promises and then feel stressed because we can't deliver. A cardinal rule of librarianship: Never promise what you can't deliver. Not only does it cause you stress, but it also harm the good relationship you have established with your customers. Retailers know that "a satisfied customer tells one or two other people; a dissatisfied one tells ten." This is true of libraries as well.

We need to learn that "no librarian in any work situation completes every single project every day. Every librarian faces, each day, a variety of priorities and projects that must be juggled" (Cochran, 11). Indeed, for some of us, this variety is one of the reasons we went into librarianship. The key is to control our feelings of frustration and anxiety, as described later in this chapter.

We also hurt ourselves by the way we think. "Did you know that 80 percent or more of your internal dialogue focuses on your shortcomings" such as negative thoughts and negative self-talk? (Davidson, . . . *Managing Stress*, 263). Too many choices or alternatives can also cause stress (Davidson, . . . *Managing Stress*, 318).

Another category of self-induced stress is physical. We don't take care of our health. We may not get enough sleep, may exercise too little, may not eat right, or may misuse or abuse drugs or alcohol. Physical stress also comes from our workplace. We may work in less-than-ideal facilities, surrounded by ambient noise (whether from other people, piped-in music, buzzing fluorescent lights, paging systems, or other sources), indoor pollution, harsh or insufficient lighting, or poorly designed furniture. We may fear for our security at work or on the way to and from work. We may suffer from eye fatigue from staring at computer screens or discomfort or pain from repetitive stress injuries. We may be crowded into isolating cubicles or asked to work in open spaces with no sense of personal space or privacy. (Although these two situations are opposite, they both can be stressful.)

There are many other stressors to deal with. We have to meet deadlines, both those over which we have control and, more often, ones set for us by others. Fear or discomfort with public speaking or other phobias can make us feel stressed. Argumentative, incompetent, tardy, disorganized or unreliable co-workers are stressful. Boredom and its opposite, overwork, are also stress-producing, as is work we just plain do not like. The organization that is in crisis due to changes in management or ownership or competition can be a stress-filled workplace. Commuting is not stress-free. It adds unpaid hours to the workday, traffic can frazzle nerves, and rushing to avoid being late is certainly anxiety-producing. Ambiguity or uncertainty—the unknown—is always a problem. And a great stressor can be one's relationship with one's supervisor. We may feel we are being treated unfairly, have to cover for a disorganized boss, are the target of hostile behavior, or just plain do not get along with him or her. Most people deal with the major stuff at work reasonably well, but "much of what bugs us on a day-to-day basis is actually the 'small stuff'" (Carlson, 3).

Library managers (including one-person or solo librarians) may be subjected to stressors unique to their level of responsibility. Davidson identifies the following ten (Davidson, . . . *Managing Stress*, 97).

1. Interruptions
2. Workload
3. Organizational politics
4. Responsibility for subordinates
5. Firing someone
6. Reprimanding someone
7. Balancing work and personal life
8. Dealing with upper management
9. Conducting performance reviews
10. Trying to work within a budget

We do not always recognize stress or realize that we are suffering from it. It is not always obvious. Davidson (. . . *Managing Stress*, 22–24) lists the following symptoms or behaviors: focusing on the trivial, absenteeism and lateness, irritability, inability to concentrate, poor attitude, depression, resentment, loss of interest in sex, clumsiness, over- or under eating, or stomach problems.

Burnout

Do You Have a Life?

Fill in the blanks. If you have trouble thinking of what to write, you are in serious danger of burnout.

"If I could reduce the length of my typical workday by having more free time after normal working hours, I'd use that time to. . ."
"If I could reduce the amount of work I normally do on the weekend, I'd use that time to. . ."
"If I knew that I wouldn't have to check my e-mail and/or voice mail and/or respond to pages while on vacation or holiday, I'd change the way I use that time off by. . ."

From Gordon, Gil. *Turn It Off. How to Unplug from the Anytime-Anywhere Office Without Disconnecting Your Career.* New York: Three Rivers Press, 2001.

One of the most severe consequences of workplace stress is burnout. *Burnout* is when a person is so stressed that he or she quits his or her job or even drops completely out of the job market. It seems an extreme solution, but it does happen. "It is important to try to prevent burnout, because it is rarely confined to one worker" (Stueart and Moran, 206). Kennedy (3) lists four stages of burnout:

1. *Enthusiasm.* The worker likes and enjoys the job and the workplace. He or she looks forward to the workday and to future years in the same position.
2. *Stagnation.* The worker has reached a plateau in the job. He or she has mastered the tasks assigned. There is little prospect for promotion or increase in pay. There is little or no job satisfaction or challenge.
3. *Frustration.* Faced with a stagnant job situation, the worker sees no way out. He or she may still be effective, however.

4. *Apathy.* Now the worker, although still going through the motions of his or her job, is ineffective and even harmful to the organization. He or she may make mistakes, bother or undermine the efforts of co-workers, or even indulge in sabotage.

Symptoms of burnout include the following:

- *Excessive absenteeism or tardiness* (due to physical symptoms, such as illness or tiredness, or due to emotional inability to face the workday).
- *Poor job performance* (due to depression, inability to concentrate, or lack of motivation).
- *Poor attitude* (pessimism; boredom; feelings of alienation; cynicism; impatience; negativism; rudeness; taking frequent, long, or unauthorized breaks; clock watching; or detachment to the point of resentment of work and the people in it).

Burnout is not about working too hard but about not being able to control when you work or spending the day doing things you do not want to do" (Louise Lague, The Wisdom Group, Greenwich, CT, in Tullier, 59). "The road to burnout is paved with good intentions. It happens when people try to reach unrealistic goals and end up depleting their energy" (Kennedy, 3). Those most vulnerable to burnout "are highly motivated, idealistic people, who often persist in trying to attain impossible goals" (Kennedy, 3).

Stueart and Moran (202) define plateauing:

Most organizations, including libraries and information centers, are now in either a non-growth or a downsizing mode. Well-qualified employees find their career advancement blocked, because there are no openings in the positions directly above them and, even worse, many of these positions are held by individuals who are only slightly older than the employee who is seeking advancement, so there is little likelihood the position will be available before retirement.

A *plateau* "is a sign of success and is to be expected not only in our professional careers but in our personal lives as well. There are two types of plateaus that we can and probably will experience in our professional lives. A *career plateau* is reached when we are entrenched in the organization's hierarchy. For whatever reason, we have gone as far as we can go within the organization. We may still have the ability to do more advanced work, but we do not have the opportunity" (George, 536). The *content plateau* "occurs when individuals lack additional challenges to expand their expertise. They have learned all there is to learn in a position and find that the responsibilities are predictable" (George, 537).

Stueart and Moran (205) say:

> The number of librarians suffering from the effects of stress or burn-out is increasing as a result of working in such an ever-changing environment. Burnout is a specific type of stress-induced condition that affects individuals engaged in "people" work. Burnout results from emotional strain and the stress of interpersonal contact, especially from dealing with people who are having problems.

Librarians, especially those working in small or solo libraries, are especially vulnerable to burnout: Their bosses and clients demand nearly instantaneous answers but their libraries have very limited resources, especially in personnel. They are "expected to do many jobs simultaneously."

However, the primary cause of burnout is overwork. "Even on a satisfying job, good stress can quickly turn bad when work hours balloon out of control" (Shellenbarger). "In mathematics, when you add and add without stopping it's called infinity. In life, when you add and add without stopping it's called insanity" (Mary LoVerde, *Stop Screaming at the Microwave: How to Connect Your Disconnected Life*, in Tullier, 58). At least in the United States, workers are being asked to work longer hours for little or no extra pay. Technology has increased both the pace of work and the amount of work output expected. There is nothing inherently bad about working hard. In fact, working hard is fine—*if* you enjoy it and are doing it for *yourself* or your *own* satisfaction. Otherwise it is drudgery. There is a difference between hard work and overwork. "Excess work hours put in by already overtaxed employees are of negative value to an organization when viewed in the context of overall work performance, direct health-care costs, and productivity lost to absenteeism and general lethargy on the job" (Davidson, *The Complete Idiot's Guide® to Managing Your Time*, 8). Even the creator of the cartoon character Dilbert, the archetypical American technology worker, agrees. "The average person is only mentally productive a few hours a day no matter how many hours are worked" (Adams, 319). From a librarian, "If you are finding you are working overtime on a regular basis, stop! If work doesn't get done, then explain that you can only get it done if you have money for additional personnel." From a *Working Smart* promotional flyer: "The danger of working in a job where co-workers try to outdo each other by burning the midnight oil is that everyone focuses on the wrong thing. Peer pressure's healthy when it's based on attaining excellence; it's destructive when it induces employees to hang around when they should be at home." Some of this extra work is "defensive overwork." Employees may be afraid that if they do not work overtime they will either lose their jobs or not advance in their careers. One of my former colleagues was told by his employer, "If you're only working 40 hours a week you probably won't be here next year."

Unfortunately, "not only has the technology changed so we *can* work almost anywhere and anytime, and employers have changed so we're *expected to* work almost anywhere and anytime—we as individuals are changing so that many of us actually *want to be able to* work almost anywhere and anytime" (Gordon, 8). Sometimes we confuse "speed of delivery with speed of action [required]" (Gordon, 33). For example, ask yourself, "If someone with whom you work fairly closely and frequently sent you an e-mail or voice mail message at 6 p.m. on a Tuesday, by what day and time would you feel you had to reply to it?" What would your answer be if it were sent at 6 p.m. on Friday? At 8 p.m. on Tuesday? At 8 p.m. on Friday? Or at 8 a.m. on Saturday? (Gordon, 32) If the answer is the same for each, you are not making time for yourself outside work hours. In addition, "The shorter the interval between the time a message is sent and the time we're expected to respond, the more pressure we feel." (Gordon, 32).

Gordon (54) tell us:

> The world, your boss, your clients, and everyone else around you aren't going away, so you have to learn to cope with (rather than hope to escape) the pressures they create. Your own desire to carve out some more free time in your life is valid and justified, but since no one is going to had you a few more unencumbered hours each day, you'll have to work out a way to make better use of the hours, days, and weeks that you have.

You are entitled to a life. In fact, you *must* have a life outside work to be a well-rounded individual.

Companies that constantly require overtime may be new startup companies, understaffed, in crisis, or show a disregard for employee working conditions or morale. The United States offers less vacation than any other country, and the gap is increasing as vacation time is reduced or the awarding of vacation beyond the basic two weeks is delayed. Austria, Belgium, Denmark, Spain, the Netherlands, and Switzerland give their employees about five weeks of vacation a year; Finland, France, Great Britain, Italy, and Germany average about six weeks; Luxembourg and Sweden offer over more than six weeks. The lowest number of weeks of vacation outside the United States was in Ireland, at 3 weeks (Schor, 82). In much of the world, we have been taught that time equals money equals good and that leisure equals bad (Schor, 7).

In addition, many people invest too much of their personal self-image in their jobs. Too many of us think that there is nothing wrong with being a workaholic. What is a workaholic? "One whose desire to work long and hard is intrinsic and whose work habits almost always *exceed* the prescriptions of the job they do and the expectations of the people with whom and for whom they work." (Machlowitz in Mackenzie, 17, emphasis mine) "Workaholics are addicted to work, not results" (Garfield in Mackenzie, 17). We also too often think and describe ourselves in terms of our jobs, saying "I am a librarian" instead of "I am a human being or wife or mother or husband or father or son or daughter."

What can the librarian do to avoid burnout? The single best way is to *just say no!* Say no to unreasonable deadlines, say no to overtime, say no to more work for the same pay or more work with the same resources. As one of the leaders of our profession says, "work hard, work well, work effectively . . . until quitting time. Then go home and enjoy the rest of your life" (White, 1990). Your mantra should be, "Don't do more: do better" (Tullier, 58). If you must work overtime—and this should be only occasionally—make sure that you are getting something out of it. You should look for, in this order, pay, promotion, catching up, or the goodwill of your colleagues or your boss. When you *do* work late, make sure that you are noticed by your boss (or your boss's boss). For instance, send e-mail or stop by to deliver something.

"Prevent burnout—the keys seem to be balance and growth" (Carlson, 239). Concentrate on the quality of your work—being efficient and effective on the job, not on the quantity of work you do. Make sure that you are judged on results, not on how many hours you work. If you are always working overtime, then you are not working efficiently, are not focused. (Dan Sullivan, trainer, in Davidson, . . . *Managing Stress*, 60). Here are two good ways to break the cycle of overtime. If you find you are staying late at work almost every day, start by saying that on, say, Tuesdays, you will leave on time and take no work home with you. Once you have been doing that successfully for a whole month, add another day. Keep it up until working late or taking work home is the rare exception, not the rule. Another idea from Davidson (*The Complete Idiot's Guide® to Managing Your Time,* 10) is to make a "dynamic bargain" with yourself. In the middle of the afternoon, ask "What would it take for me to feel good about ending work on time today?" Then do it, and leave on time.

Law librarian Chris Graesser suggests five ways to conquer burnout: "bond with your colleagues"—network in and outside of the library, "get the hell out of Dodge"—change jobs, "get a life"—focus on getting enjoyment out of non-work activities, "your best interests are not the same as your employer"—stand up for yourself, and "know thyself"—make sure you and your job are suited for each other.

Hemphill and Gilbard (23) write that the simple answer to overload is to trade work with colleagues; a simpler answer is to hire a temp or outsource the work; and the simplest of all? Get rid of nonessentials or push back a deadline. Davidson (*The Complete Idiot's Guide® to Managing Your Time*, 8–9) suggests finding role models—successful people within the organization who work close to "normal" hours. Scott Adams, the American cartoonist and business satirist, has written of his new corporate concept, OA5 (Out at Five)—"the perfect company." "The primary objective of this company is to make the employees as effective as possible . . . employee effectiveness is the most fundamental of the fundamentals." "The goal of my hypothetical company is to get the best work out of the employees and make sure they leave work by five o'clock" (Adams, 318–320). Finally, here are some other ways librarians can avoid falling victim to burnout. These suggestions are specific to burnout. For more ideas, see the next section on dealing with stress in general.

- If you have too much work, ask your boss for help. If you cannot find help within the organization, see if some of the work can be shifted to another department, outsourced, or eliminated. Use the alliances and partnerships you have formed within your organization or in the greater library community. Network.
- Set limits on how much you will work and keep to them. Advice columnist Ann Landers said, "No one can take advantage of you without your permission."
- Know yourself and the pressures you put on yourself. Set reasonable goals—that you can reach. "Don't accept undoable jobs."
- If you are bored or need a challenge, ask for more work or take on something new. Restructure your job Change departments or bosses. Change jobs. Serve on a company-wide committee or task force and meet new people. Look at your job. Is satisfaction there somewhere? "In case you haven't figured out the main ingredient to staying the same profession at the same place for almost a quarter of a century and still enjoying the job, it's *change!*" "Take risks. Volunteer to investigate and develop new library services." "Learn new skills." "Keep up with new trends." "Get involved [in your professional associations]" (Slyhoff, 581).
- Get active professionally. Volunteer at the local, regional, or national level in your professional association. Run for office.

- Learn something. Take a course at a local college or university—or on the Web. It does not even have to be related to librarianship.
- Take a vacation. Many people do not take all of their vacation—make sure you are not one of them. Along the same lines, take all of your breaks and lunch hour. Get out of the office for lunch.
- Have a life outside work. Find unstructured, noncompetitive hobbies. Spend more time with family and friends. Take time for yourself.
- Re-evaluate your priorities and take a look at your options. What do you really want out of your job and your life? Make a strategic plan for both, with written goals.
- Let go. "Can't Get Caught Up? Just Quit! No, I don't mean quit your job. I mean quit trying to get caught up. I'm sorry to be the one to tell you this, but it will never happen. As you already know, the job of a librarian is never done" (Bacon). Or, as a law librarian put it, "I learned long ago that my professional work would never be done or caught up. So why work fourteen hours a day, seven days a week? Balancing the work I get paid to do with the other things I love to do is a great stress-reliever. My job is not boring because I look for ways to force myself to learn what is new (or my students or staff or colleagues force my hand!) and try to apply that in the day-to-day world. And because I refuse to let my job, alone, define who I am" (Hazelton, 567).
- And the best suggestion of all? "Find your bliss in your work and in your leisure and find a synergy between them" (Bausch 542–543). Work your joy! (If you don't enjoy your job 99 percent of the time, find another job that you *do* enjoy.)

Avoiding, Minimizing, or Eliminating Stress

Obviously, many, if not most, librarians enjoy their work. Why else would they work for the low pay that they receive, in a profession that suffers from a public relations problem, and such demanding clients?

J. Wesley Cochran

This quotation goes to the heart of the problem of stress. On the one hand, we are doing work we love. On the other hand, we are under stress. How do we reconcile these two issues? How do we make it possible to continue to do our jobs without destroying ourselves? There are four major ways to deal with stress:

1. Change the way you think.
2. Change the way you work.
3. Take it easy.
4. Plan and prioritize.

Change the Way You Think

You can surrender to the fact that work is inherently stressful and there's nothing you can do about it, or you can begin to walk a slightly different path and learn to respond in new, more peaceful ways to the demands of work.

Richard Carlson

All too often librarians labor under two major misconceptions: We have to answer every question for everyone and we have to be perfect. As noble as these ideals are, they are just plain wrong. There is no way we have the time or resources to help everyone who comes into our library with all their information needs. And no one is perfect. As one author put it, "Remember, whatever happens, you're doing fine" (Boorstein, 23). Other unrealistic attitudes that need to be avoided include "needing unanimous approval, believing events should turn out the way you want them to, thinking people should always respond the way you expect, expecting to win all the time, and believing past bad experiences will determine future results" (Hemphill, 99).

Another fact of life is that sometimes good enough is good enough. "Not all tasks you encounter require 100-percent effort on your part for you to achieve completion!" (Davidson, . . . *Managing Stress*, 193). This applies to internal documents, memos, drafts, and minor research, among others. "A project that is 90–95% correct may require 50% of the original time to do the last 5–10%—and that 5–10% is the most stressful. Decide if that last 5–10% is worth the time and stress" (Davidson, . . . *Managing Stress*, 193). (This is another application of the 80/20 rule.)

Lighten up; have a sense of humor. Don't take yourself too seriously. Do what you enjoy—at work and elsewhere. If you don't enjoy what you're doing, you shouldn't be doing it. Remember the Golden Rule (Do unto others as you would have them do unto you)? A Canadian business librarian suggests, "Put yourself in others' shoes and remember to say please, thank you, etc. and be pleasant. It doesn't help your stress level but it will help your colleagues and there will be days when they will return the favor." Carlson (227) advises, "Forgive yourself: You're human" (227). And Porat (61) asks, "Do you praise yourself enough?" Another liberating idea comes from Boorstein (17). Be open to new ideas. "Don't plan for any particular results. Who knows what new view is just around the corner? Being on the lookout for something specific might divert us from seeing something really great."

Think positively. For instance, don't say, "I hate to go to work" or other negative statements. Carlson (282) suggests several positive steps. "Don't live for retirement"; live for today. Join the TGIT club— "Thank God It's Today" (39–40). "Marvel at how often things go right" (233). Problems are the exceptions, not the rule. "Stay focused in the now" (80). However, it is important not to dwell on the past; we must not become so now-focused that we forget to look back at how far we have come. Make a "past accomplishments" file. "It is uplifting to look back at a list of your past triumphs. It gives you a sense of perspective when you start thinking you aren't getting anywhere" (Silber, 133). On the commute home, think only about what you did well that day. Banish negative thinking: Be aware of how often you think negatively and how counterproductive it is. Write down negative thoughts, and look at them logically. Do a reality test on them. What is the worst that can happen? Reprogram yourself to replace negative thoughts with productive and realistic thoughts. Move from "poor me" to "I'm in charge of my own life."

Don't worry. Worrying is a waste of time. In fact, "the very act of worrying, particularly about something distant in time or about which one has little control, inhibits good time management" (Cochran, 79). Do what you can and let the rest go. "Don't sweat your critics" (Carlson, 270). "Accept the fact that there's almost always going to be someone mad at you" (Carlson, 156). Accept Murphy's Laws, which are:

- If anything can go wrong it will—and at the worst possible moment.
- Nothing is as easy as it looks.
- Everything takes longer than you think.
- Left to themselves, things tend to go from bad to worse.
- If there is a possibility of several things going wrong, the one that will cause the most damage will be the one that goes wrong.
- Corollary: Murphy was an optimist.

Back off when you do not know what to do. Inspiration may come to you. "Say 'I don't know' when you don't" (Pollar, 63). It's no sin to be ignorant; the only sin is to pretend you know the answer when you don't or to give a wrong answer just to avoid saying that you don't know. My father the engineer always said that there were only two answers to any question: the right answer or "I don't know." (The day I started library school that changed to the right answer or "I'll find out.") "Acknowledge and honor your feelings" It's okay to be angry, upset, sad, whatever. Ask: "Is this worth making myself sick over?" (Marshall J. Cook, 191–194). Don't get mad. Don't get even. Just get on with it. If it helps you, plan an escape route—an alternate plan. For instance, count down the days to something pleasant. Tell yourself that everything is temporary. (Only death is permanent.)

Give yourself permission to fail. Failure is all right if you learn from it, if you failed because a higher-priority task came up, or *if* you did not get the resources you needed (such as cooperation from someone else). In fact, if you have not failed, it means you have not risked, not challenged yourself.

Dr. Albert Ellis has written extensively on living rationally in an irrational world. I have found his observations and advice very helpful, both personally and professionally. Central to his philosophy is that "You feel the way you think" (Ellis and Harper, 8). Observe your feelings, acknowledge them, determine their appropriateness, then choose to feel what you want to feel (29). Ellis wrote about a series of "irrational" ideas. Here are a few that I think have special application to librarians.

Irrational Idea No. 1: "The idea that you must—yes, must—have love or approval from all the people you find significant. Adults do not need approval" (Ellis and Harper, 88). We cannot please everyone and should not even try to do so.

Irrational Idea No. 2: "The idea that you must prove thoroughly competent, adequate and achieving [all the time]" (Ellis and Harper, 102). We should do our best but not strive for perfection at all times. It is neither possible nor necessary.

Irrational Idea No. 6: "If something seems dangerous or fearsome, you must preoccupy yourself with and make yourself anxious about it" (Ellis and Harper, 145). What possible good can come from worrying about things that may or may not occur?

Irrational Idea No. 8: "Because something once strongly influenced your life, it has to keep determining your feeling and behavior today" (Ellis and Harper, 168). "You make yourself happy or miserable by your perceptions, attitudes, or self-verbalizations about these outside events" (33). The past is just that, past. It should no longer affect our thoughts, attitudes, or actions.

Finally, "no absolute shoulds, oughts, and musts exist in the world." If you believe that they exist, then you "claim God-like powers that you do not possess" (Ellis and Harper, 79). Get rid of them. There

is only one thing you *have* to do in this world. You have to die. This is
from an anonymous source:

> Mr. Meant-To has a comrade,
> And his name is Didn't-Do;
> Have you ever chanced to meet them?
> Did they ever call on you?
> These two fellows live together
> In the house of Never-Win,
> And I'm told that it is haunted
> By the ghost of Might-Have-Been.

Change the Way You Work

*No one should become consumed by a job or a company; earning a
living is an important part of life, but not the only important part.*

Hyrum A. Smith

Do not let your job define your life. We are people, mothers, fa-
thers, sons, daughters first and librarians second. You are a librarian
because you chose to be one. Find another job, if you find it too stressful or are unhappy. (This includes griping about low pay, lack of pres-
tige or respect, problem patrons, and so on.) "Having an extraordinary
amount of responsibilities and obligations in your personal and professional life is nothing to brag about. Don't make the mistake of judging
your or others' self-worth by how much you have to do. Truly accomplished people have balanced lives, not overextended ones" (Tullier,
35). "If you are killing yourself by taking on too much, you will not be
productive in any area" (Weeks, 73). Leave work at work. "On your
way home from work, select a point along the [way]. In your imagina-
tion, dump each day's stresses at that same spot" (Pollar, 107). Think
about this, do you really have to do all that you do? An independent
information broker says: "Try not to dwell on [your time management
problems]. It does no good to moan about being 12 years behind on
reorganizing the files. Break things down into small pieces or projects.
Celebrate small victories and accomplishments."

Change how you react to situations at work. "Focus on the problem
at hand, rather than getting bogged down in politics, personality or ego
issues" (Shellenbarger). Don't nurture grudges. "Don't sweat the bu-
reaucracy." Just accept that it exists and try to make peace with it
(Carlson, 27). "Don't let negative co-workers get you down" (Carlson,
220). Deal with problem co-workers by either accepting them or find-

ing help in changing the situation. Don't obsess about deadlines (or anything else). Just deal with them. "Believe it or not, you're not indispensable. Not to the world. Not to your country. Usually, not even to your company. . . . Don't overestimate your own value and worth" (Davidson, . . . *Managing Stress*, 77). But don't *under*estimate your worth either.

Don't take responsibility for failures that are not of your own doing. Barclay says:

> If you blame yourself when things go wrong at work it can make you more vulnerable to illness. . . . increased job demands in those who feel inadequate to handle them may translate into more colds, flu and other infections. Levels of [infection-fighting] antibodies were lowest in those employees who believed they had control over their job responsibilities, but lacked confidence in their problem-solving abilities and blamed themselves for bad outcomes.

Avoid feeling powerless by informing yourself about the situation [preferably in advance] (Davidson, . . . *Managing Stress*, 202). Knowledge is power.

"Let go of lower-level decisions as often as possible. Let someone else choose when the choice is of no [or little] consequence" (Davidson, . . . *Managing Stress*, 318–319). Few decisions are irrevocable. "Grief over past mistakes in unproductive. Learn the lesson and move on" (Pollar, 77). "Let go of battles that cannot be won" (Carlson, 150). Distinguish between problems you can solve and those you cannot. Remember the Serenity Prayer. (Grant me the Courage to change what I can, the Serenity to accept what I can't change, and the Wisdom to know the difference.) Be less controlling. "To be controlling means you are preoccupied with the actions of others and how those actions affect you . . . the trait of being controlling is highly stressful" (Carlson, 8).

Find easier ways to do things. If you feel guilty because "everything" isn't getting done, eliminate things from your "must-do" list. Emphasize self-service by being proactive with bibliographic instruction and handouts. Make a handout or a sign for questions that come up frequently, or create a library frequently asked questions (FAQ) list on the organization's Intranet. Outsource what you can. (Follow the rule, "Don't do what you can buy," for instance, cataloging and interlibrary loan.) Delegate when appropriate. "Learn to let go of the unimportant things. If your job requires you to stay on top of the latest advances in engineering, don't sweat it if you can't name the top ten movies of the past year" (Davidson, . . . *Managing Stress*, 138). (One of Judy's Laws of Librarianship: Don't memorize what you can look up.)

Let go; don't be a perfectionist. Remember, you do not have to be perfect—only good. Sometimes "done okay" is better than "partly done but perfectly." In the same vein, resist the temptation to do small, insignificant tasks too well (*e.g.*, making the monthly report a literary masterpiece). When you outsource or delegate, however, do not be overly critical and do not micromanage. Choose the best providers or employees, and let them do their work. If you look over the provider's shoulder constantly, you will not be saving your time. "Make allowances for incompetence." A certain amount is unavoidable. Taking it in stride is not the same thing as condoning it (Carlson, 162).

Pedley says:

> I am a perfectionist. I like to get things right. But I have to reconcile this with managing my time as effectively as possible. When I write an article or a book I set myself deadlines, and do everything I can to make sure that I am able to stick to those deadlines. I like to check my work, and to read it over and over again until I am happy with it. But in order to ensure that I am not going to waste any time, I set myself a deadline and use that as the cut-off point. I know that I am never going to be 100% happy with a piece of work and therefore I may as well set myself a specific point in time at which I will just have to accept that there is no more time to keep going back and revising the text. So, to manage your time effectively, you have to be quite ruthless.

Handle conflict appropriately. "Conflict in work relationships is the biggest cause of stress in workers' lives" (Clark and Clark, 275). "The more responsibility you assume, the more chances for conflict increase. Conflict is normal and should be expected" (Clark and Clark, 276). But don't overreact or obsess about conflicts on the job. Stress can also result from the seemingly conflicting roles we are asked to play, such as serving users vs. managing others, concentrating on high-priority projects vs. interruptions, or dealing with the present vs. planning for the future (Walster, 3–4).

There is *always* an alternative to a stressful work situation. "Whenever a situation becomes intolerable there are three choices open to all of us: to escape the situation, to change the situation, or to change the way we view the situation. It is up to you to choose which is the right way for you" (Kennedy, 5).

According to Clark and Clark (275), in coping with conflict, you can back off, become indifferent, make concessions, go to a third party, become enemies, or problem-solve. If you are having problems with your supervisor, find safety in numbers, make sure you do not pass the problem on to others, or find out what organizational resources are available to help you. If you are involved in a disagreement with a colleague, "take note of what's [really] being said" (Carlson, 203). Did you maybe misunderstand?

Do you feel angry at your situation? We are usually angry because our goals, values, expectations, or self-worth have been attacked. "If you really want to control your anger, though, figure out how to use it as an ally" (Murphy). Tap into it to speak out on behalf of your library or yourself. Using your anger does not mean becoming violent or even writing a nasty note. If you are really upset with your current situation, use that anger to change it; make it better, or find another job. Divide what makes you angry into two categories: those you cannot do anything about (forget these) and those you can (the fuel for change). "The next time you're angry about an incompetent co-worker or a nasty boss or a dead-end job, ask yourself a question: What good can come out of this?" (Murphy).

"Finally, accept that there will be days that you will not or cannot do the things you feel you should or could have done. No matter what happens, simply resolve to keep trying" (LeBoeuf, 3).

A paralegal and information specialist says:

> I've learned to accept that I'm not indispensable, and that I cannot be everyone's hero all of the time. I can only manage my time, my life. Once I realized that, I stopped feeling obligated to accept every task and to promise that every request would be completely satisfied before end of business. I do accept almost all of the tasks that come my way, but I've leaned to share my turf with others, and to delegate aspects to support staff.

Take It Easy

When faced with a stressful situation, apply the strategy of the pause. Pause, breathe deeply, survey your options, think about the consequences, then—and only then—act (adapted from Davidson, . . . *Managing Stress*, 199). If you feel overwhelmed, take a break. "When you're in a stressful situation over which you have no control, stop a moment. Take a deep breath. Acknowledge that you've done your best. Turn your mind to how to salvage the situation, instead of fuming about what's already happened" (Davidson, . . . *Managing Stress*, 190). Take time to think: "You need time to figure out where you are—with a project you're in the middle of, with the direction your career is headed, with the course your life is taking. It's because we haven't had time to think that we've allowed our work lives to get so out of control"

(St. James, 27). Don't worry. Worry leads to paralysis, which leads to incomplete work, which leads to worry. If you insist on worrying, give yourself five minutes to fret, then get on with it. "Spend ten minutes a day doing absolutely nothing" (Carlson, 207). It calms you down, allows you to see things in a new light. It allows you to imagine and dream. Marshall J. Cook (45–48) identified "seven ways to go on vacation without leaving your desk":

1. Two minutes of deep diaphragmatic breathing.
2. Two minutes of thinking of your ideal place—a tropical island, for instance. (McGee-Cooper, 97: "We have learned that the very act of anticipating something we enjoy changes the chemistry in our brains and gives us wonderful benefits.")
3. Picture your problem, then picture yourself destroying or smashing it.
4. Rotate your head and shoulders.
5. Read a quotation, a bit of humor, wit or wisdom, something in fiction, something not work-related.
6. Look at a picture of a person or object you love.
7. Or any other relaxation technique you find that works.

Avoid creating stress by pressuring yourself. Do something easy—a quick win—it will change your mood for the better and defuse stress. Be aware of the stress you feel. Be realistic; do not set unrealistic goals. Learn to say no. Pace yourself. The world will not come to an end if something does not get done today. Know when to quit. More is not necessarily better.

Davidson says that multitasking is "Good for Machines, Bad for Humans" (Davidson, . . . *Managing Stress*, 99). Too much multitasking can lead to frustration or burnout (Tullier, 60). "Others who know you are a master juggler have a tendency to keep throwing things at you. Make sure you're juggling your staff, not somebody else's" (Silber, 73). Debra Wood (49) says:

Technology encourages people to take advantage of every moment. Rather than spend a few minutes to unwind or pull thoughts together, people convert time in a taxi or airport into productive minutes. But such capabilities foster what Rosen and Weil [Larry D. Rosen and Michelle M. Weil, authors of *TechnoStress: Coping with Technology @WORK@HOME @PLAY*] call "multitasking madness." Rosen reports that multitasking eventually catches up with everyone, even the early adopters who do it well. Multitaskers discover they have difficulty concentrating and sleeping soundly.

While this all is probably true, it is not realistic for most librarians. Therefore, it is especially important for us to be aware of how multitasking can cause stress and make sure stress does not get out of hand.

Take one thing at a time. Look no further than the next step. (This is how I managed to climb down the very steep and high Mayan pyramids, even though I am very uncomfortable with heights.)

A corporate librarian says:

> Take care of yourself both physically and emotionally. Exercise. Eat right. When you're stressed, do something physical: take a walk, get a drink of water (not coffee or tea—the caffeine can make things worse), sit very still, get up and move around, do some quick exercise, stretch in place, or try relaxation breathing. Emotionally, compose yourself, think happy thoughts, or try meditation. Don't allow others to burden you with their stresses to the point that you get short tempered, work overtime consistently for no extra pay, or become resentful.

Ask yourself, "What would a calm person do?" (Davidson, . . . *Managing Stress*, 307).

"Accept the fact that, every once in a while, you're going to have a really bad day" (Carlson, 95). Just go with it. It's not the end of the world. You will survive. If you think of your everyday problems as only speed bumps, they are easier to take (Carlson, 88).

Sometimes just talking to yourself, out loud, helps clarify things or release stress (Davidson, . . . *Managing Stress*, 275). Speaking up for yourself also helps; keeping everything in will make you miserable. However, don't overdo it. "Even merely discussing your stress can add to it" (Davidson, . . . *Managing Stress*, xxiii).

Plan and Prioritize

The best way to handle stress, of course, is to avoid it in the first place. And the best way to do that is by advance planing. As Davidson (. . . *Managing Stress*, 332) says, "Contingency Planning—A Real Stressbuster." Planning can range from sophisticated long-range strategic plans to simply deciding what you're going to do in the next hour. For instance, on the way to work, think about and plan what you want to do for that day. Start this as soon as you leave home. Get into "work mode." On the way home, go over what you accomplished and what you want to do tomorrow. And, very importantly, when you get home, stop thinking about work and get into "home mode." Leave the office at the office.

Plan for disasters, even for minor ones. Ask yourself the following questions. "What's the worst thing that can happen in this instance? So what? Will it mean the end of the world? (So far, I haven't found a situation in which the answer to that last questions was "yes.") What will I do if it does happen? How will I recover? What will I do next? If you think these things through, when the worst *does* happen, you are prepared. You have a plan. You will not be as stressed as those without a plan.

The constant interruptions that librarians encounter have potential to cause great stress if not handled properly. First, accept that interruptions are inevitable. In fact, if no one interrupted us with questions, we probably would not have jobs. Second, deal with the interruption and then go back to your highest priority. If possible, ask the interrupter if he or she can wait until you get to a convenient stopping point. If you are in charge of the decision process, you will feel less stress.

Planning alone is not enough. Since we cannot do everything that's asked of us or even everything we want to do, we have to decide what we will do. We must decide what's important to us, to our libraries, and to our organizations. Decisions about our family, home, or career are more important than deciding which movie to attend, what to have for dinner, or which suit to wear. Don't spend an inappropriate amount of time on low-priority decisions. Don't stress yourself out over them. Important things should have a high priority and take most of our time and attention. Those things with lower priorities can be left for later or perhaps not done at all.

Information overload is also a cause of stress. We seem to have either too much information or too much general information. We have to sift through it to get to what we need. It is impossible to know everything and, in nearly all instances, it isn't even necessary. The same is true for our clients. Very few people want *all* the information on a subject—they just want enough information to make intelligent decisions. (Exceptions might be in the area of patents, medicine, and some scholarly research.) Making sure you know how much information your client wants will eliminate the twin worries of not finding enough information and finding too much.

Do you know the priorities of your organization? Of your boss? Of your boss's boss? Your priorities and those of your library should dovetail with theirs. As will be dealt with in greater detail in Chapter 5, priorities are not constant. They change often and sometimes unpredictably. "A workplace with shifting priorities is a situation where you probably have very little control, and the only workable response is to flow or adapt" (Cochran, 35). Priorities often conflict; handle conflicting priorities or bosses with communication. Get the bosses together with you to discuss and negotiate their priorities for you. They may not even be aware that you're overwhelmed. Boorstein (15) says:

> We certainly could have been better prepared [for life]. Mostly, we do it without an instruction manual. Mostly, it's a surprise. It's usually what happens when we are planning something else. Maybe it's *always* what happens when we are planning something else. We manage anyway.

4
Strategic Planning

Libraries rarely plan. Instead they react to what others have already decided in such areas as budgets and staffing and then "plan" to make the best of the situation.

Herbert S. White

Failing to plan is planning to fail.

A common saying

Have you ever heard the saying, "If you don't know where you're going, any road will get you there"? or "If you don't know where you're going, how will you know when you get there?" Planning is the answer. By deciding what it is that you want out of life, you can decide how to get there. The same is true for your library.

Planning also allows you to focus your thinking on the future. People (and especially OPLs) often get so caught up in the moment, fighting fires and keeping their heads above water, that they forget about the future—where they are heading. Planning also saves time, fights uncertainty, helps you focus on your objectives, and is critical for efficiency. In other words, planning equals control.

Up to this point, this book has dealt with various time management techniques; however, this chapter is about the most important time management tool of all—planning. If you have a plan and know where you are going, you can direct your efforts to the most important activities. You do not waste time on unimportant tasks. As Mackenzie (28, emphasis his) said, "*Planning* your day, rather than allowing it to unfold at the whim of others, is the single most important piece in the time management puzzle." "Given the importance and ubiquity of information and knowledge today, strategy and strategic plans are more—not less—important to librarians" (Jacobson and Sparks, 15).

What Is Strategic Planning?

The simplest definition of *strategic planning* is that it is a structured way of dealing with the uncertainty of the future. Corrall's definition is a bit more detailed:

> Strategic planning is essentially a process of relating an organisation and its people to their changing environment and the opportunities and threats in the marketplace; it is a process in which purposes, objectives and action programmes are developed, implemented, monitored, evaluated and reviewed . . . . [It is] particularly concerned with anticipating and responding to environmental factors, taking responsibility for change, and providing unity and direction to a firm's activities. It is a tool for ordering one's perceptions about future environments in which one's decisions might be played out Alternatives [are] a set of organised ways for us to dream effectively about our own future.

"A plan is a goal, indicating certain beliefs; a schedule, specifying steps to be taken; a theory, considering relationships; and a precedent, established for existing decisions" (Cyert and March, 111–112, in Stueart and Moran, 36). Stueart and Moran (36) say:

> Planning is both a behavior and a process; it is the process of moving an organization from where it is to where it wants to be in a given period of time by setting it on a predetermined course of action and committing its human and physical resources to that goal. Basic questions of *who, what, when, where,* and *how* are prepared by the most important philosophical question of *why*.

"According to Peter Drucker (121–122, in Stueart and Moran, 41):

> Strategic planning is the continuous process of making entrepreneurial—or risk-taking—decisions systematically and with the greatest knowledge of their future consequences; systematically organizing the efforts needed to carry out these decisions; and measuring the results of these decisions against the expectations through organized, systematic feedback.

In "Planning and Evaluation: The Endless Carousel," Herbert S. White (38) correctly describes planning as a *proactive process*. Both terms are important. By planning, an institution develops both a vision of the future and a strategy for controlling it. This enables the employees to anticipate rather than react to events in the future. In addition, the planning process itself is very important. Properly done, the employees in the institution develop and agree on common goals; that is, they make sure they are on the same wavelength and are moving together in the same direction and toward the same ends. Although the usual end result of strategic planning is a document, the best results are obtained because of the process. "Because planning is a delicate, complicated, time-consuming process, it cannot be forced on an organization that is not prepared for self-analysis and the change that will result from the process" (Stueart and Moran, 37).

Libraries and their parent organizations often are rather conservative and risk-averse. "Strategic planning is most appropriate for use by these conservative organizations" (Riggs, 3). Your strategic planning process must interact with or mirror that of the parent organization. It cannot be done in isolation. The library must be seen in its context—the company, the law firm, the hospital, the community, the university, and so on. "People who work in small libraries . . . can use the planning process as an opportunity to get closer to customers and involve them in discussion about the library's future" (Corrall, 6). "Planning has become a major preoccupation for library and information services managers. Many information units in business and industry are struggling to justify their existence" (Corrall, 1). Although special libraries have known this for years, libraries in other sectors (such as public and academic) are starting to find this out. The existence of a library is no longer a certainty. This is where a well-thought-out and well-implemented strategic plan can be important.

What strategic planning is *not* (adapted from Allison and Kaye, FAQ, 15):

- It does not predict the future. Decisions are made in the present.
- It does not make decisions that cannot be changed. If assumptions change, plans can change.
- It is not a substitute for judgment—it is a tool.
- It is not always smooth or linear.

Is strategic planning the same as long-range planning, goals, mission statements, or visions? Sort of. The difference between strategic and long-range planning is emphasis. Long-range planning often takes several years. In a special library you do not *have* a year to create a long-range plan, five to ten years to achieve it, or decades to realize a goal. At best you might have a month to create, a year to achieve. (Five

years is a lifetime!) Goals, mission statements, and visions are all part
of a strategic plan. But the plan encompasses more than just goals, missions, and visions—much more.

Before we go any further, it is a good idea to define a few terms.

Definitions

Here are some definitions related to planning that you should know
(adapted from McCuistion).

Planning: An organized process for anticipating and acting in the future in order to carry out the library's mission. It involves development of alternative scenarios and action plans.

Strategic Plan: The plan that focuses on the library's overall direction
and fundamental mission (and that of parent organization, if any).
It typically covers a period of three to five years (or more) and includes all operating units of the library.

Vision: A concise statement of what the library would like to become in
the future. It should be so idealistic that it is not attainable in the
foreseeable future.

Mission: A relatively short, clear statement of the primary purpose(s) of
the library. It consists of the library's reason for being, what it
does, how it does it, and how the library is different from its competitors. The mission should reflect the library's values or the basic
beliefs to which the library and its stakeholders have agreed. It
may be achievable in the midterm.

Goals: Statements of specific items that the library wants to achieve.
Developed from the Vision and Mission Statements, Goals must be
measurable and able to be completed by a specified date.

Strategies: Action plans that are formed in the planning process that
constitute how the library will accomplish its vision, mission, and
goals. These may be either long-term (strategic) or short-term (tactical).

Stakeholders: Any or all of the individuals or organizations that are
affected by the actions of the library. Although they do not determine policies or goals, their needs and opinions should be taken
into account. They may include, but are not limited to employees,
users, nonusers, management of the parent organization (if any),
vendors and suppliers, and the community at large.

Tactical Plan: The plan that covers primarily the first year of the Strategic Plan and the action plan for implementation of the goals and
objectives of the library. These are short-term strategies.

SWOT Analysis: A technique for analyzing the environment in which the library operates or may operate in the future. It includes the following:

    Strengths: Areas in which the library has strong capabilities or a competitive advantage, or areas in which the library may develop capabilities and advantages in the time period covered by the Strategic Plan.

    Weaknesses: Areas in which the library is lacking the capabilities necessary to reach its goals, or areas that can be expected to develop within the time period covered by the Strategic Plan.

    Opportunities: Situations outside of the library that, if capitalized on, could improve the library's ability to fulfill its mission. These may exist now or develop within the time period covered by the Strategic Plan.

    Threats: Situations external to the library that exist now or may develop in the time period covered by the Strategic Plan that could damage the library and should be avoided, minimized, or managed.

Why Plan?

"Why plan? The short answer is that planning helps us to prepare for a better future; it is good management practice, and is often an organisational requirement" (Corrall, 3). What will the future bring for your library? What do you want it to bring? If there is going to be any chance for the future to turn out the way you want, you must plan. If you do not plan the future of your library, someone else will. And it is not likely to be the future you envision.

    Berner says of planning:

> Without a sense of where you want to go, how can you ever know if you are going in the right direction? Without planning you merely struggle through the day-to-day operations of the library—relieved no doubt, to get through each day—but you never bring your library any closer to realizing its ultimate goals. How can you if you have no idea what those goals are? Yet isn't that movement toward specified goals—for our libraries, for our parent organizations, and for ourselves—one of the things that marks us as professionals? Without it we are really nothing more than clerks. The most often-heard cry is, "but I don't have time for planning!" I can only respond by saying you'd better find the time. Doing long-range planning will give you the direction you need for intermediate planning and for short-term planning. Before you know it, you'll have a sense of direction which

may have been lacking in your work before. Suddenly you'll find that you can be making decisions about the work you do (e.g., do I really need to do this?) rather than simply filling your day with tasks that seem to have no purpose.

Unfortunately, libraries rarely plan. Instead they react to what others have already decided in such areas as budgets and staffing and then "plan" to make the best of the situation. Proper planning, by contrast, is a proactive process." (Siess).

In addition, "planning helps you to get the *right* things done" (Cochran, 28, emphasis mine). If you don't know where you're going it doesn't matter which road you take. In addition, "it doesn't matter how long it takes to get there" (Mackenzie, 24). In 1980, Porat (xii) said, "One problem in American commerce, industry, and corporate endeavor, is that we are so busy with the present that we do not leave time to plan the future." Twenty-odd years later this still holds. In fact, planning is probably even more important today.

Strategic planning is also a valuable management tool. Planning is about managing change. It reinforces the role of the library in the organization, improves the image and visibility of the library, and can demonstrate the librarian's competence and professionalism. Planning can help support your case for funding. It keeps you on course. Planning also gives the staff an idea of where the library is going, thus helping assure their commitment to the library's future.

Why don't we plan? According to Mike Higgins, author of Beyond Survival (in McCuistion), most managers and board members do not know how; many organizations are doing very well today and feel that "If it ain't broke, don't fix it"; they've never done it; they are intimidated because there is a fear that they might lose their job if anyone finds out that they have not been doing a good job based on new measuring criteria; planning takes time, and time is a precious commodity indeed in today's environment; and planning costs money because there typically is an off-site planning session plus the hiring of a professional facilitator.

Steiner (63–64) listed four approaches to planning:

1. Top down: Does not involve line staff, but provides more control.
2. Bottom up.
3. A combination of the first two.
4. A team approach.

The best approach usually is one of the last two. Another good approach to strategic planning is "goals down–plans up" (Corrall, 7).

The planning process is as important as—or maybe even *more* important than—the product. But it must be an iterative, interactive process. Everyone that has a stake in the library must be involved. As Beckwith says, "The greatest value of the plan is the process, the thinking that went into it" (61). In addition, strategic planning can be used when the organization is contemplating a change in direction or to rejuvenate a tired or staid organization, or to improve communication within an organization. Unfortunately, some organizations engage in strategic planning exercises just because "everyone" is doing it. This is not a particularly good reason for initiating a strategic planning project; however, if this is what it takes to get you started, then it is good enough.

Cochran (18) wrote, "Librarians, as a group, appreciate the value of planning." However, smaller libraries often fail to understand the value of the process. "The best way to assure we have quality libraries well into the future is to continuously reinvent and revitalize them. . ." (Himmel and Wilson, 4).

Strategic planning creates confidence by the parent organization that the library knows where it is going and how it will get there. It can also improve prospects for future funding. The process improves staff morale and motivation, helps make them less reactive, and instills in them team spirit and a sense of community and corporate identity due to a shared purpose. As decisions are dispersed downward, staff may experience more job satisfaction. And improved staff morale leads to improved customer satisfaction. More relevant and effective services and faster responses are other benefits of the strategic planning process. This process allows the library to take advantage of new technology as it becomes available, because current and future needs are known. Wide distribution of the strategic plan creates a higher profile for library and staff and opportunities to influence decision makers.

You say, "I don't have time for this"? Well, you had better make the time. How else can you decide what to do and, more importantly, what *not* to do? Silber (23) writes, "Don't tell me you're too busy to plan. If you don't plan, you'll be busy without accomplishing much." "You don't have to go so fast if you're going in the right direction—and then you have time to enjoy the ride." In other words, you don't have time *not* to plan.

People give all kinds of reasons for *not* planning. Here are a few: I don't know how. "If it ain't broke, don't fix it." It's always been done this way. It's expensive. It will limit my flexibility and creativity. I will be locked into the plan. I could be fired if I don't stick to the plan. It won't help me handle my everyday workload and the inevitable emergencies. It will just create more paperwork for me. It's hard work.

Do you think planning for the future is a waste of time in these times of rapid change? Eric Lease Morgan ("Springboards for Strategic Planning," 32) responds:

> In a time when change is the norm, describing the future of anything seems a bit ludicrous. Similarly, planning may seem to be a waste of time. You might say, "How can I make plans when I have no idea what is going to happen in the future?" It may seem ironic, but these are the exact times when planning, specifically strategic planning, are most beneficial.

Ulla de Stricker (28) adds, "without strategic planning, few of us will succeed. . . ."

Have you ever gotten to the middle of a project and found that you do not have something you need to finish it? Pedley (4) says:

> Only by putting down on paper the steps that are involved can you begin to identify potential problem areas, such as: Are the key people going to be on holiday just at the time you need them? Is the equipment double booked? Do you need to book some training as part of the project [but] the consultants need 2–3 months' notice ahead of running a training course for you?

How will you ever find the time to plan? How about on the way to work or at the beginning of your workday? You might need to come in early, because planning at the end of day usually is not effective. Once you have done your strategic or yearly plan, do not just forget about planning. Set time aside every week for planning. You may need to go somewhere quiet, away from the library.

One of these days is none of these days.

Old English proverb

In the long run, men hit only what they aim at.

Thoreau (in Cochran)

If a person aims at nothing, he will probably hit [nothing].

J. Wesley Cochran

How to Plan?

Now that you know what planning is and how important it is, you need to know how to do it. De Stricker describes six steps in the process:

1. "Taking Stock: Perception, Other Players"
2. "Identifying Stakeholders and Understanding Their Priorities and Plans: Preoccupation"
3. "Creating Products to Match the Priorities: Product, Place, Price"
4. "Communicating to Stakeholders: Press, Promotion, and Pushing"
5. "Provoking the Sale"
6. "Getting and Using Feedback: Probing and Polishing"

Jacob (13) divides the process into three phases:

Phase 1: "Analyze the current situation of the library, the parent institution and their environments" (the strengths and weaknesses of the library and its parent organization and identify problems, needs, concerns, and ambitions).
Phase 2: Create a vision of the library's future.
Phase 3: Implement the plan: Translate broad goals into tangible results.

Another method for starting the planning process is the Merlin Method described by Lemberg. "Legend says Merlin was born as an old man and lived his life growing younger." He did not really predict the future, "he was simply relating events which for him had already happened."

1. "Begin at the end, *having realized* your intentions. Ask the following questions.
2. What did you have to do *just* before you reached your goal? What *resources* did you need? What *skills* did you need to acquire? What did you need to know?
3. And, what did you have to do just *before* that?
4. Do Steps 2 and 3, coming forward in time, until you reach the beginning."

Riggs (44) calls this the "backward analysis" approach. Decide where you want to be at the end of the plan, then work backward to the present. How will you get from here to there? Stephen Covey (35–36) suggests that you "begin with the end in mind. Start with a clear understanding of your destination. Know where you're going . . . so that the steps you take are always in the right direction." You want to learn everything possible from your previous actions, results, and mistakes, and you want to resolve old issues. For instance: What were your goals? What did you actually do? What did you not do, and why? What did you do right? What did you do wrong? Still another view of the planning process is shown in Figure 4.1.

I have chosen to use the model proposed by a nonlibrarian. Marketer and inspirational speaker Harry Beckwith created a great outline for planning—The Three Cornerstones.

1. Predict the future.
2. Decide what you want your future to look like.
3. Analyze the results.

To these I have added one more, without which the planning process is merely an academic exercise.

4. Implement the plan.

Before you even begin to plan, there are a few things you need to do. It is extremely important that everyone who has a major stake in your library has bought into the process (i.e., agrees to its basic assumptions and goals). Involve users and management. It might be a good idea to involve *non*users as well. Do not forget the staff. Involve them in strategic planning. It helps them to understand why change is needed and gives them a personal stake in it. You also will get suggestions from those on the front lines; listening to and implementing them helps create a team (Corrall, 5). Besides, those who are going to implement the plans should be involved in the planning.

Make sure that both you and your staff understand the purpose of planning and have the same expectations as to what it can—and cannot—accomplish. Make sure everyone is willing to question the status quo and try new approaches. Riggs (19) says that individuals not committed to the planning process should be excluded from it, if possible. I am not sure I agree. Everyone should be included, if only to be informed. They may become committed later. If you exclude them, there is no chance of their buying into the plan. When forming your planning team, ensure that you include the minimum number of people that can be on the team without endangering its success. Nelson (19) suggests that 9 to 15 committee members will usually "work well," but Steiner (18–19) says that in no case should there be more than 12 people in the planning session. You may want to prepare a document for the members of the planning committee. You will want to include the following: the reason the planning process was undertaken, the process itself, the approximate time it is expected to take, how much of the committee's time it is expected to consume, and brief biographies of the other committee members.

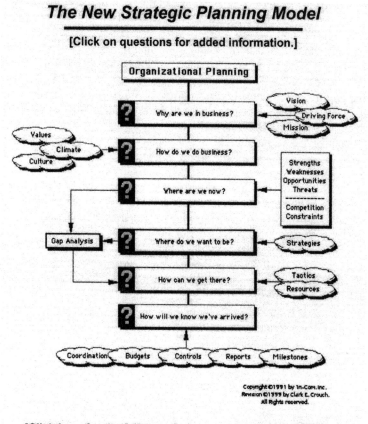

Figure 4.1. Flowchart of the Planning Process by Crouch. (From http://crouchnet.com/planning.html [accessed 20 May 2001]. Used with permission.)

Before starting to work on your strategic plan, you should ask yourself the following questions:

- Whose idea was this?
- Why are we doing this?
- What is the most important outcome of this planning process?
- What other positive outcomes are likely?
- What is the down side, and how can it be eliminated or minimized?
- What are the consequences of *not* planning?

Consultants can aid or guide the planning process but should not do the planning—that must be done by library management. The positive aspects of hiring a consultant are that he or she is trained to make the group work effectively, has confrontation management skills, is not distracted by content issues, and usually is perceived as neutral in the event of conflict. On the down side, it may be difficult to find the right person, or the facilitator may require education in jargon, content, library issues, and community issues. In addition, hiring a facilitator can be expensive, and concerns over confidentiality may arise. If you are going to hire a consultant, make sure that he or she is on the same wavelength as are you and your staff. However, the library director has the ultimate and overall responsibility for the strategic planning process and must be actively involved at every stage of the process.

You are going to have to have some brainstorming sessions. Here are eight rules to guide the process:

1. Be creative.
2. Never criticize anyone's ideas.
3. The more ideas the better.
4. Build on the ideas of others.
5. Do not stop to discuss or explain ideas.
6. Do not edit—record all ideas exactly as stated (very important).
7. Take turns; try to contribute one idea each time it is your turn, but pass if you have no ideas.
8. Have fun.

In addition you will need to resolve any current major crises and internal conflicts that exist. Unresolved conflicts will distract everyone from the process and may influence the results. Make sure there are enough resources (time, people, and money) available to complete the entire process. You will need to collect and analyze a substantial amount of information, and this takes a lot of resources.

The library *must* have the support of its parent organization. If the parent has a strategic plan, the library's should be part of it or at least should follow a similar format. Your most important stakeholders are "those who look after the strategic direction of the entire organization" (de Stricker, 30). Be sure that you inform and involve the staff and stakeholders before, during, and after the process.

Jacobson and Sparks (15) say:

> There is no magic wand to wave that will instantly produce a strategic plan. Instead, it takes a lot of hard work. Moreover, and much to the chagrin of the planning side of the process, the most difficult work begins *after*, not before, the plan is completed. Getting direct and indirect reports, customers, and suppliers on board with the plan is a long, arduous process, particularly where significant change is involved.

Here are a few final tips for a successful planning process (Silber, 60–62). Visualize the outcome you want; define it clearly. Gather your tools and information before you start. Brainstorm without judging. Be flexible: If one approach does not work, try another way. Anticipate problems and delays, and develop alternatives and "escape routes." Estimate how long each step or phase will take. Set a firm but realistic deadline.

A Sample Planning Time Line.

Task	Approval Points	Action	Date
1	Yes	Design process	Month 1
2	No	Orientation meeting	Month 2, week 1
3	No	First planning meeting	Month 2, week 2

Leave time for thinking, reflection, and evaluation of progress so far. Make sure every task is really necessary. To this I would add, do not bite off more than you can chew. Focus only on the most important issues in your strategic planning. "There are only a few critical questions which the plan needs to answer. If you don't have any important choices to make about your organization's future, you don't need a strategic plan" (Allison and Kaye, FAQ, 3). Remember to include cost-benefit analysis in your strategic plan so you have facts to support your decisions.

Talk with other librarians about what they have done. "Don't dismiss what happens at different-sized libraries, or at different types of libraries. All libraries do essentially the same things" (Bremer, 8). But be aware that "techniques that work well in one particular library may not work well in another" (Cochran, 13). Resist the temptation to borrow someone else's plan nearly unchanged. Your library is unique and so should be its strategic plan.

Finally, here are some Planning Do's and Don'ts by Nelson (42, 62, 90, 130):

- "Don't assume you already know everything there is to know about your [user] community."
- "Don't write more goals and objectives than you can manage in this planning cycle."
- "Don't forget that you asked the planning committee to make recommendations and that you need to take those recommendations seriously."
- "Do be sure that planning committee members clearly understand the implications of the priorities they are recommending."
- "Do assure the library staff that changes will be implemented over a period of time and that appropriate training and resources will be available."
- "Do select measures that are time- and cost-effective."
- "Do be open to new ideas when determining which community needs the library can help meet."
- "Do encourage staff to be creative when identifying possible [ways to meet service needs]."
- "Don't assume that you can obtain new resources to accomplish all of the new things in your plan."
- "Don't collect more data than you need to make . . . decisions."
- "Don't underestimate the effect the plan will have on the 'way we've always done things here'" [or the effect that way of thinking will have on the success of the plan].
- "Do remember that the key to effective resource allocation is to estimate, implement, check, and adjust."
- "Don't assume that staff will automatically integrate the activities in the new plan into their daily routines."
- "Don't hesitate to make changes in the plan when circumstances change."

Cornerstone 1. Predict the Future

"Planning is an effort to anticipate the future and the inevitable change that comes with it. It must be accomplished by choosing from among possible alternatives, and with full knowledge and use of techniques and tools available for such action" (Stueart and Moran, 53). This is hard. Eric Lease Morgan (33) says:

> Few, if any, people successfully predict the future with 100 percent accuracy, but there are experts who have wider perspectives than the rest of us and, consequently, are more apt to see what lies ahead. Librarians of the future will always be keeping one ear tuned to the experts and one ear tuned to their individual experiences. Use what you hear to plan your future. Your vision may not be the one everybody else sees, but at least it will provide a framework for future decision making, and will enable you and your library to evolve with our dynamic professional environment.

However, "forecasting helps reduce uncertainty because it anticipates the results of a decision about a course of action described in the forecast. Forecasting is the most valuable planning technique. It attempts to find the most probable course of events or the range of possibilities" (Stueart and Moran, 53).

Before you can predict the future, you should examine the past and the present. In planning strategy, we are trying to convert information and knowledge to a decision about a course of action in the future. We can only have information and knowledge about the past or present. The future is not known; it exists only in our minds. We can decide what we will do—our strategy—but we cannot guarantee that the world we knew and the world we predicted when we choose a course of action will be the same when we are actually carrying out those actions. Hence, even during the implementation of strategy, we cannot escape the continuing need for thinking" (Wells, 9).

What is the history of your library? Of the parent organization? How did you get to this point? What did last year's Strategic Plan say? What did you accomplish? Where did you fail? What do your users want? What are their needs—and dreams? What does your boss or organization want? What do *you* want?

Now you must examine your library's environment. This step is usually called an *environmental scan*, but has also been described as a *situation audit* by Steiner or *taking stock* by de Stricker. What is involved? You need to answer the following questions.

- What do you mean by "library?" Ruth Fraley (3) writes: "The number of things called 'library' has grown exponentially. Do library plans include the technology department? Records management? Archives? Instructional technology?" The library is no longer limited to a physical location; it can be virtual—on the users' desktop, on the Web, or the organization's Intranet.

- What is the organizational culture of the library? Of the parent organization? What are the unwritten rules and mores? Is it a formal or an informal organization? Is there a culture of sharing, or are units pitted against each other? How does information flow? Is it top down, bottom up, horizontal, or is there no consistent pattern? From where does the library's support come? (Include both financial and moral support.) Do you know where the organization is going and where its leadership *wants* to go?

- Who are your customers? Who are your potential customers? What are their opinions of the library and its staff? Have these opinions changed recently? Why? Which of your services do they deem most valuable? Which could they do without? Do they even know there is a library? If not, why not? Who does not use the library? Why? This is more than asking what your customers want. They may not know what they want today (or, more importantly, need) and are very unlikely to know what they will want or need tomorrow.

- What does the top management of your organization think of the library? Do they even know it is there? Do they use it? "Could you identify the top three concerns of your CEO [Chief Executive Officer] or General Manager today? How about the CFO [Chief Financial Officer] and COO [Chief Operating Officer]?" (de Stricker, 30). Does the organization have a CIO (Chief Information Officer)? From which department did he or she come? Is this a possible career path for you? (If not, why not?)

- Who are your competitors? From where else can your users obtain information? What are the sources of information for your nonusers? How did they manage before the library was established? Could they manage without the library? Think about positioning yourself in the market, not in terms of how you think but how the customer thinks. "Who else in the organization is doing something others compare with (or confuse with) what we do" [such as information technology (IT)]? Do automation vendors call on IT instead of the library? Do vice presidents consult the library first, or do they go elsewhere? Does the head of the library have a title and rank comparable to other department heads?

- What information do your users actually need? Include both print and electronic information—and do not forget nonwritten (verbal) information. How does the informal network or grapevine work? Is the library in the loop? In which format or formats do your users prefer to receive their information? Is e-mail a viable delivery method?
- Are there any mandates to the library from outside the organization? These mandates may come from accrediting bodies or boards, customers or members of the parent organization, or even the public.
- What are the economic constraints under which you can expect to work? Is the organization growing or contracting? Is it profitable? For a not-for-profit organization, find out if the budget is growing, if donations or membership are increasing. Can you expect additional staff in the future—or might staff cuts be more likely?
- What kinds of technology are already installed? What technologies are expected in the future? Is your organization likely to adopt them? (That is, is it an early or late adopter of technology?)

You also will need to do an in-depth analysis of your library itself. How does your staffing relate to the needs of your users? If you find you are understaffed, could improvements in staff training or efficiency make up the difference? Ask the same questions about space and equipment—could greater efficiency be achieved? Look at all library reports, policies, and procedure manuals. Review any other library strategic plans that have been done. If staff turnover has been a problem, consult the personnel department to determine the reason(s). Compare your facilities, services, staff, and funding with other libraries in similar organizations. Take inventory of what you already have (books, journals, and staff) and what your users—and nonusers—want (Bremer, 29). "Smart managers *do* collect a lot of input, but they use it as context within which to make their own decisions, not as a popular vote" (Bergonzi, 26).

Nelson suggests that when analyzing or describing your library, you may want to include the following:

- *Users and Population:* number of users as the percentage of the total population, users by department, users by class (administrators, managers, technical staff, clerical, other—compared with total population).
- *Total Population:* potential users not on-site, evaluated the same way.
- *Availability:* hours open, hours staffed.

- *Employees:* number of employees (in full-time equivalents [FTEs]), number of professionals, paraprofessionals, clerical staff, volunteers, other (and number of hours worked by each class).
- *Resources and Materials:* data for five years ago, now, and estimated for five years from now; comparison to other similar libraries: by subject, medium (books, video, slides, microfilm, CD-ROM, photos, journals, and so on).
- *Technology:* Internet access (number of terminals, usage), electronic databases (number of services, number of sources covered, availability on desktop or in library, usage, cost).
- *Networking:* associations belonged to (cooperatives, consortia), ILLs sent and received, cost.
- *Physical Facility:* size, condition, appearance, location, equipment: carrels, book stacks, photocopiers, fax machines, and so on.
- *Financials:* budget by subject (materials, technology, staff, training and development, reference).
- *Statistics:* circulation, reference transactions, attendance at training sessions, searches (by Internet, online, CD-ROM); do these by department, subject.

DeGennaro proposes three strategies for forecasting (in Stueart and Moran, 54):

1. *Deterministic:* This strategy assumes that there is a close causal relationship between the present and future. This strategy places great reliance on information about the future.
2. *Symptomatic:* This strategy searches for signs that might be indicators of the future, for example, the Leading Economic Indicators. This approach is based on the concept that the sequence of events in a cycle is a consistent pattern.
3. *Systematic:* This strategy looks for underlying regularities over a period of time. Econometrics is an example of this type of forecasting. Riggs (20–21) divides the analysis process into two areas: external elements (users and nonusers, new technologies, competition) and internal elements. The latter includes comparing the resources and performance of your library to those of similar libraries and other units in the parent organization, the makeup of the user population, the degree to which the library meets user needs, and the resources available to you. Koch (21) also divides analysis into two categories, but his two are the majority, which has little impact, and a small minority, which has a major, dominant impact. This is the 80/20 rule at work again.

The most common way to evaluate an organization is by SWOT analysis—strengths, weaknesses, opportunities, and threats. See the definitions at the beginning of this chapter for more on this technique. Other common evaluation techniques include the following:

- *Peer Comparisons,* also known as *benchmarking.*
- *Sector Analysis:* used to measure customer service, this involves analyzing your industry, technology, publishing, resource-sharing, site visits, and printed reports.
- *PEST Factors:* political factors (*e.g.,* government, regulation, industry situation, taxes), economic factors (employment, exchange rates, inflation), societal factors (target audience, staff skills, managerial style, and technology (installed base, internal and industry standards).
- *Determinants of Service Quality:* This method can be very time-consuming. Although it may use anecdotal evidence, or stories, it primarily consists of measuring the following: reliability (consistency, dependability), responsiveness (willingness, readiness), competence (skills, knowledge), access (approachability, convenience), courtesy (politeness, consideration, friendliness), communication (understandable language), credibility (trustworthiness), security (physical safety, financial security, confidentiality), understanding (knowing the customer, listening, individualization), and tangibles (facilities, equipment).

How do you gather this information? Scrutinize both the library and its parent organization. Read any and all reports, old planning documents, and strategy documents that you can find. Talk to library staff and other employees who have been with the organization for a long time to make sure you understand the history of the institution.

The temptation is great to use surveys to gather a lot of information very easily and quickly, but can you rely on this information? Those people most likely to return a survey may not be the ones from which you most need a response. The busiest employees will not take the time, but they are likely to be the organization's most productive or valuable and therefore the ones who can benefit most from the library's services. They are also most likely to be nonusers of the library. You can make a survey very short or use check boxes to increase responses, but you will lose the best information that way. If you choose to use a survey, be sure to include some open-ended questions and follow up as many surveys as possible with interviews.

The best method by far is the interview. This does not mean merely asking random employees, "What do you think of the library?"

You need to be methodical and specific. Unless your organization is very small, you cannot interview everyone—nor should you. You do not need to have a statistically significant stratified sample, but you do need to make sure you have all the bases covered. Include users and nonusers, management and line staff (perhaps even the cleaning staff). Do they know that the library exists? Do they have an opinion about your service?

In addition to asking the usual questions about desirability of and satisfaction with current library services, you should encourage "thinking outside the box" or what I call "blue-sky thinking." Ask questions such as, "If money were no object, what would you like the library to do for you?" This is a very hard thing for most people to do, conditioned as we are by the constraints of reality, but it will give you an idea of what the library *could*—and maybe *should* do. (Be sure to remind your interviewees that you are making no promises of future services.) You should also ask them: "Have you ever *not* searched for information because you thought that you would not be able to find it, or that it would take too long or cost too much? What was that information? Did not having the information have an impact on the decisions you made or the progress of the project?"

You may need a slightly different strategy for upper management. Become "comfortable asking a senior executive to lunch in order to discuss matters of mutual concern" (de Stricker, 29). The questions you ask also should be different. De Stricker (30) suggests three:

- What do you care about?
- What goals and projects are your priorities?
- What do you see as major time wasters?

If you do not know what your boss expects of you, make an appointment and *ask*. Present what you think your top three goals are, or what you want them to be, and get his or her input. If your boss does not have time to meet, keep at it until he or she does meet with you.

The planning process in not-for-profit (NFP) organizations such as libraries may be different from the process in other organizations. "Planning in the NFPs is a much more complex process than in the private sector" (Steiner, 321–324). It is more political, especially in government; more influenced by outside constituencies; may not have as clearly stated missions, goals, and objectives; may have a more complex and subtle purpose (the public interest, not profit); and may not have as clear or direct a chain of command. Libraries are very formal in hierarchy and communication channels. Librarians tend to follow old habits and procedures. Strategic planning, when taught in library school at all, usually refers to public or academic libraries. Planning materials specific to libraries are hard to find. Steiner (335–336) lists the following "Overarching Lessons of Private Strategic Planning Experience Applicable to Planning in the NFPs." Customize the process. It must be a joint effort of line and management. The organization must have a planning-friendly climate. Do not expect too much. Do not confuse the plan with too many goals or goals that are too vague; keep the process simple.

Cornerstone 2. Decide What You Want Your Future to Look Like

Now that you know where you have been and where you are, your problems and assets, the needs of your users and the organizational culture you work within, it is time to start describing where you would like to go and where you would like your library to go. Then you can begin to map out ways to make sure your future comes out the way you want. Corrall (31) describes the process as follows:

Vision (Where do we want to be?) + *Values* (How do we want to do things?) = *Mission* (What is our business? Who are our customers?) → *Objectives* (Why are we here? What do we do?) → *Goals* (Where are we going?) → *Strategies* (How will we do it?)

The Vision Statement

"A vision . . . is a clearly articulated statement of what you wish your institution to become, i.e., a future-oriented statement" (Penniman, 51). It should express your aspirations, core values, and philosophies. Your vision should be very general and not achievable—at least in the near term. The lifetime of a vision is at least five years and can be much longer. It should be stated in the present tense and be short— seven words or less, according to Clark E. Crouch in "The Terminology of Strategic Planning." Remember that your vision is the desired future state, based on the most probable scenario. It should be idealistic, inspirational, exciting, and challenging. Another word for *vision* is a *dream*.

To achieve your vision, share it with the participants (staff, customers, and management). Let those affected read the plan, or even help write it. Make use of your library committee, focus groups, and surveys. "Use what you hear [from experts and your own environment] to plan your future. Your vision may not be the one everybody else sees, but at least it will provide a framework for future decision making, and will enable you and your library to evolve with our dynamic professional environment" (Morgan, "Springboards," 33).

Here are some sample vision statements (Corrall, 23–24):

- "The world's leading resource for scholarship, research and innovation" (The British Library).
- "A leader and innovator in university library and information services" (Aston University Library).
- "Unity with diversity, open communications and trust, collaboration, innovation, initiative" (Harvard College Library).
- "Seven institutional values" (U.S. Library of Congress):
    1. The best service feasible.
    2. The best quality feasible in every aspect of its activities, large and small.
    3. Ensuring all library activities are designed to accomplish its missions; achieving optimal results through efficient use of resources.
    4. Constantly seeking, testing, and employing new and creative methods.
    5. Fairness to staff and users.
    6. Encouraging widespread staff participation in the planning, implementation, and ongoing evaluation and improvement.
    7. Staff excellence, leadership development, individual growth, job satisfaction, and opportunities for career development.
- "To help one-person or solo librarians around the world by informing them and championing their cause" (Information Bridges International, Inc.).

The Mission Statement

People often confuse vision and mission statements. The main difference is that a mission is achievable. Penniman writes that "[A] mission [is] a statement of 1) what the institution does, 2) for whom it does it, 3) how it does it, and 4) why." It should contain measurable objectives and targets. It also "defines in broad terms the enduring fundamental and distinctive purpose of the organization and its role in the community—what it is trying to accomplish" (Corrall, 21).

The mission statement can be longer than the vision statement, but still should be relatively short—one hundred words or less. In addition, it should be unambiguous and understandable, reflect consensus, accepted by the stakeholders, measurable, achievable, concrete, concise but complete, memorable, and relevant to the mission of the organization. It should be simple and user-friendly. If a library serves more than one clientele, the mission statement should state the different services or levels of service to each clientele.

A mission statement should *not* "be a detailed laundry list of library services, be a multi-paragraph, multi-page statement, be continually modified, or reflect only today's goals" (Jacob, 61–62). Its life span is shorter than that of the vision—three to five years—but it should reflect the unchanging values of the organization. Of course, there are other opinions. Cartoon character Dilbert defines a mission as: "a long, awkward sentence that demonstrates management's inability to think clearly" (Adams, 36).

Here are some sample mission statements (Corrall, 24–26):

- "Integrity of the collections, strong user focus, creativity and innovation, organizational flexibility, caring for the needs of the staff" (Massachusetts Institute of Technology Libraries).
- "To anticipate, determine, stimulate and satisfy the needs of existing and potential users for access to information in an ethical manner." Information and Library Services Lead Body (the UK Development Body for Standards in Library Science). Corrall suggests that this "can also be viewed as a generic mission statement for libraries."
- "To bring the latest personal and institutional management information to small (especially solo or one-person) libraries around the world" (Information Bridges International, Inc.).

Objectives

The next step is to define your objectives. Objectives are statements of intent: Why are we here? What do we do? Objectives are often confused with goals (see the next section, Goals), but they are not the same. Objectives are the environmental scan put into short, specific, measurable statements. They are suitable to and supportive of the mission of the institution and need to be acceptable to those involved. (All who are affected should agree on them before you go on to the next step—setting goals.) Objectives also must be achievable, flexible, motivating, and understandable. They should state what you intend to do, how you will know that you have succeeded, and who is accountable. Timetables and dates for completion should be discussed but will be added at the strategy-setting stage of the planning process.

Bremer (2) cautions us: "[a] formal, long range, thoughtful plan requires a full year to create. Achieving the objectives listed in the plan may take from five to ten years. Realizing a goal may take decades." It is highly unlikely that you will have a year to work on your plan, and even less likely that your organization will allow you five to 10 years to achieve your objectives. However, they will take time. Be patient, and be prepared for obstructions and even failures.

Goals

After you have defined your objectives, you can then set your goals. Goals are objectives made real. They are "long-term objectives that guide your daily decision-making. They are the accomplishments by which you judge whether you have achieved success. Goals are necessary to effectively focus your time and energy on the task at hand" (Allen, 22). They are one way—and a very powerful way—to motivate yourself to greater accomplishments. Another name for goals is a "service response," that is, "what a library does for, or offers to, the public in an effort to meet a set of well-defined community needs. They represent the gathering and deployment of resources to produce a specific public benefit or results" (Nelson, 8).

But "no one ever met a demanding goal without devoting time to it" (Mackenzie, 24). "Many people do not really set goals. Only about 3 percent of the general population actually conducts a planned, purposeful goal-setting session" (Weeks, 21). Why? First, it takes time. Second, goal-setting can be seen as scary. "A goal is a planned conflict with the *status quo*. By definition, then, reaching a goal means doing something new, leaving familiar, comfortable terrain of our comfort zones and exploring new frontiers" (Stanley Smith, 79).

Several writers describe goals as being SMART:

- *Specific:* Goals should be clear, not vague or abstract.
- *Measurable:* so you know that you have achieved them. Be sure to congratulate yourself when you reach them—even reward yourself. "If you don't measure it, you can't manage it" (an old saying). Jacobson and Sparks (20) say:

> Senior management, as well as your own managers, need to know how you are performing according to plan—whether you are on target to hit your milestones, what has changed in the environment that may require adjustments to the plan, and what resources need to be applied and where to get things back on track. Particularly as a support unit within a larger organizational environment, you need to demonstrate how you are doing relative to your goals and objectives, and ultimately show the value you are creating for the firm. Metrics go to the heart of the question: is your work making a real difference?

> Suggestions: identify at least one measure for every objective. Define measurable target points, such as 95% of reference requests delivered within 24 hours. Keep it simple. Communicate expecta-

tions clearly to those who must fulfill them. Revise the system where necessary (when it is found to be too difficult to measure or circumstances change—not where you do not like the answers).

- *Achievable:* unlike vision or mission statements.
- *Realistic:* Make sure they are practical and feasible. You should have a reasonable expectation of meeting these goals, given the budget you are seeking. Ask yourself: Can we afford it? Do we have the time? "You can [and must] insist that there is a firm relationship between resources and objectives [goals]. If management insists that the funds are not there, then objectives must be modified" (White, "Planning. . . ," 39). Make sure that all members of a team understand and agree on their goal. "In a perfect world, the organization's long-range goals would be made known to all employees and all bosses would use those corporate goals to set the department's priorities and clearly communicate those priorities to everyone" (Mackenzie, 29). Even if complete disclosure and agreement is not possible, it is worthwhile to come as close as you can.
- *Timely:* that is, with a deadline—a date to start or finish. This keeps you moving forward and helps stops procrastination.

Mackenzie (32–34) adds that goals should be:

- Predetermined—"You don't shoot first and then call whatever you hit the target";
- Demanding—the most important quality;
- "Agreed to by those who must achieve [them]"; and
- Flexible—but "don't be too quick to lower your goals."

In addition, put them in writing so you can review them. "If your goals are only in your head, they're not goals. They're *wishes*" (Silber, 250). This is from the I Have Goals Web site:

The act of putting your goals in writing accomplishes two things. First, in order to be able to put them in writing you have to first think about what you want to write. So the process forces you to focus on what you really want. And when you make your goals specific and think about a target completion date, you automatically begin to think about how you will go about achieving the goal. Secondly, once your goals are in writing you will, consciously and sub-consciously, begin to make decisions on a daily basis that will move you toward achieving your goals.

If you achieve every single goal every single week and month, then you are probably not stretching yourself enough. If you are not achieving very many of your goals at all, then maybe you have bitten off more than you can chew.

Keep your eye on your goals. It is easier to determine what is important in the short run when you know what you want in the long run. Ask yourself: If it doesn't help to get you where you want to go, is it really necessary? "Everything that happens after identifying the value proposition should be about creating a 'strategy-focused organization (SFO)'" (Jacobson and Sparks, 17). Relate current products, services, skills, and technologies to each strategic objective.

Here are some sample goals.

A. Annual:
    1.   Read four new books (one each on searching, Web sites, management, and the subject matter of my company).
    2.   Take all my vacation.
    3.   Take at least two continuing education workshops.
B. Monthly:
    1.   Put finishing touches on the Web site.
    2.   Make a list of all file folders.
    3.   Sign up for a continuing education event coming up in the next six months.
C. Weekly:
    1.   Send e-mails to people I met at the conference.
    2.   Clean out one file drawer.
    3.   Move the files on my desk off my desk.
D. Ongoing:
    1.   Empty e-mail in-box daily.
    2.   Be on time for all appointments.
    3.   Check my calendar before saying "yes" to anything.

Once you have determined your goals, you are ready to set *priorities*, which are ranked goals. Then relate daily activities to goals and priorities. Finally, list the resources you need to meet these goals. Resources are not just about money; resources include staff, equipment, technology, space, coordination, and authority. Yes, I know these all boil down to money, but think in broader terms. Ask if these goals are consistent with the goals, objectives, and policies of the library. Are the goals in line with what is going on outside the library? In the parent organization? In the profession? In the world? Does the library have the resources (people, equipment, and money) to support them? Can they be accomplished within an appropriate time frame? Will they work?

Can they be accomplished? Will they produce favorable outcomes? Do they account for external factors and changes? Are they free of conflict with other areas? Are they free of excess risk?

Nelson (57) created a needs decision tree, which may help you decide if you want to include specific goals.

First ask, "How well suited is the library to meet this need?"

If it is well suited, then ask, "How many competitors are there for meeting this need?"

If there are many competitors, consider using or working with one of them instead.

If there are only a few competitors, give serious consideration to making this a library priority.

If it is poorly suited, again ask, "How many competitors are there for meeting this need?"

If there are many competitors, do not make this a library priority; use one of the other services instead.

If there are only a few competitors, this is a good goal for the library (but not necessarily a high-priority one).

Riggs (32–33) describes three types of goals for libraries; he was writing about public libraries, but these are applicable to special libraries as well:

1. *Service Goals:* include service levels, users served, and types of services.

2. *Administrative Goals:* deal with organization, coordination, and cooperation.

3. *Resource Management Goals:* cover three areas: collections (weeding targets, acquisition policies, materials availability, and delivery time), staff (productivity, morale, training, and conditions), and facilities (accessibility, automation, adequacy, and use).

Goals can also be developed from the answers to these questions (You did ask them in the environmental scan, didn't you?):

- Which user complaints didn't you resolve?
- Which requests weren't you able to fill?
- Why don't nonusers use the library?

- What could you do to draw them in? (This is a good time for blue-sky thinking. Think not only of the possible but the impossible, and see if you can make it happen.)
- Which of your current services need to be continued?
- Which can be discontinued?
- Which new services do you want to add? Why? How will the organization benefit from them? Do not add or continue an ineffective service. When considering a new service, consider the intangibles.
- Will the new service excite your potential users?
- Will it generate interest from those who fund your library?
- Does it have a good chance of success?
- Is it past-, present-, or future-oriented (future-oriented is best)?
- What are the risks associated with it? (Does the upside exceed the downside?)

Go ahead and include some items from your wish list. Not only does doing so show that you are a forward thinker, but it also gives the powers-that-be something to cut (so they feel they have fulfilled their fiscal responsibilities).

Table 4.1. Model of how to determine your objectives and goals. (Adapted from Bremer, 69.)

	Completion Date
Objective 1	
Goal 1	
Task 1	
Result desired	
Resources needed	
Task 2	
Result desired	
Resources needed	
Task 3	
Result desired	
Resources needed	
Goal 2...	
Goal 3...	
Objective 2...	
Objective 3...	

Finally, write down the prioritized goals with a general approach for achieving them. List the key tasks required to achieve the goals, resources needed (money, people, and equipment), and measures of success (evaluation measures). Remember to make these measures specific, for example, "increase circulation by 10 percent," and not just "increase circulation." After developing preliminary goals, allow *all* the library staff to review and comment on them. Make the appropriate changes, then allow administrators to review and comment on them (if required). Again, make changes. Then finalize and establish deadlines for your goals, and designate the people responsible for each step. Table 4.1 shows a model you can use.

Strategies

Strategies, sometimes called action plans, are the final step in the planning process. Here is where you write down the specific steps you will take to carry out the above. Make the desired outcomes more specific, go over the completion dates to make sure that they are reasonable and that there are no conflicts among them, and add strategic checkpoints—stoplights where the progress of the plan is evaluated and changes made if necessary. Finally, describe how you will know when you have met the objectives. When setting deadlines, allow time for unexpected problems. This will reduce stress. Think about what other milestones must be met first. To estimate the time to complete a project, make a list of *all* the parts of the project (research, an outline, phone calls, data collection, evaluation, the rough draft, critiques of the draft, the final report, and so on). Decide how long each task will take, add them up, and *double* the result. "Things always take twice as long to complete as you think they will" (St. James, 43–44). You should "try to finish projects just in time—on time, but not by much" (Stanley Smith, 42). If you complete a project too quickly, you may miss late-breaking information. Also, it may just encourage management to set shorter deadlines in the future. You will want to schedule as much as possible as early as possible to avoid running out of time.

"Project and normal work goals are written on paper (rather than carved in granite) because as needs, wants, possibilities, priorities, and resources shift, you can expect to rewrite goals and milestones to clarify and communicate the changes" (Williams, 95). There are many types of strategies, including organizational, personnel, growth, opportunistic (to take advantage of new ideas), innovation (the drive to be new *and* different), financial, and retrenchment (downsizing) (Riggs, 49–50).

Cornerstone 3. Analyze the Results

The next step is to use your previous work to develop alternative futures for you and your library. This is also called scenario planning. "In scenario driven planning, managers develop scenarios, or stories, to design possible futures. Using these stories, managers can then design strategies that will help move the organization forward." It also "lends itself to today's uncertain environment and offers managers a flexible approach to viewing the future." "Scenario planning is not an attempt to predict the future." "Any prediction of the future is shaped almost totally by our perceptions. Organizations are typically unprepared for future events because of the limitations of their perception, not a lack of effort at trying to forecast what the future might be" (Willmore, 25). Scenario planning can be used for both broad and narrow strategic planning. King (4–5) wrote about three kinds of futures: the probable, based on the past; the possible, where surprises are anticipated; and the preferable, or idealized states. All scenarios must be plausible and reflect strategic priorities and external pressures. "Additionally, scenario planning is not an attempt to develop possible scenarios for every potential development that might occur. Not only is this typically a waste of time, it leads to superficial analysis and we fall victim to our perceptions" (Willmore, 25).

King (8–15) goes on to describe eight steps for developing scenarios:

1. "Identify the central point or decision to be made" (King, 8). The why or the motivation. For example, how can we serve our users better? "The scenario planning process starts with a focal point: an issue on which it is important to develop insight. The focal point is future oriented. . . . It is often phrased as a question" (Willmore, 25).
2. "Identify the key forces in the environment" (King, 10). Are they cost, competition, staff? You will also need a complete list of the resources available to you. "A library has three types of resources that it can allocate—time, people, and money" (Bremer, 6). Crouch adds property and technology to this list.
3. "List and analyze those important driving forces" (King, 11). What is their probability? Identify trends or rate of change. Are they controllable?
4. "Rank the forces" by importance or by uncertainty (King, 12).
5. "Choose the main themes or assumptions to develop the scenarios" (King, 13).

6. "Create or develop the scenarios" (King, 13). This should include two to four scenarios with different, plausible, outcomes. They should be "structurally different," not just minor variations. One should "challenge conventional wisdom."

7. "Look at the scenario implications" (King, 15). Are they applicable to other situations? Do they clarify the choices to be made or provide new insights?

8. "Identify indicators that will help in monitoring changes as they develop" (King, 15).

Corrall (20) adds a few more hints for scenario planning. Select conceptual thinkers for the team; this should be a creative and imaginative exercise. Involve a variety of stakeholders; you should have representatives from management, staff, and the user populations. Finally, do not put all the desirable outcomes in one scenario and all the undesirable ones in another. Mix them; be realistic. However, White ("Planning. . . ," 39) says, "It is acceptable for us to present alternatives in a way to encourage approval of our recommendations." But do not make the alternatives so opposite that the "right" choice is obvious. Both alternatives should be plausible, although one may be a bit more probable and preferable than the other. In other words, do not stack the deck.

Writing the Plan

Now it is time to write your strategic plan to show how you will respond to and flesh out the mission statement. You *must* produce a document from the planning process. "It doesn't have to be polished, it doesn't have to be pretty, but a document is a symbol of accomplishment and a guide for action" (Allison and Kaye, FAQ, 3).

Steiner (60, 62) suggests that before you write the plan, you write a planning manual. It can be anything from a few pages to a 200-page document. It might include the following: an introduction describing the importance of planning and the purpose of the plan, background information, instructions to the participants, planning assumptions, a glossary of planning terms, and a bibliography. The foregoing assumes there will be a relatively large group writing the plan. In a small library, this is probably not possible or even desirable; however, you should have some sort of a document to give to those who may be helping you, outlining the process and your expectations for the final document.

The core of the strategic plan consists of the following:

- Your vision and mission statements.
- A summary of environmental forces and market trends.

- The key objectives and priorities of your plan, with annual, measurable, library-wide goals and objectives. Describe where you are now and where you want to go.
- The human resource strategy and financial projections. Include resources needed, such as staff, money, and technology, along with where they will come from. Do not plan for a specific technology; rather, plan for a specific mission and a specific vision, and then use the available technology to fulfill your mission and vision. Include information on costs and funding. (Where will the money come from? How will it be used? How much will you need?)
- A time line for the implementation of the plan.
- The ways in which you will allow for feedback, evaluation, and adjustments to the plan.

If you have the time and interest, you can add an introduction, a list of organizational values, supporting strategies, statistical appendices, performance indicators, a review of progress to date, background and overview (Who was on the committee? How did it reach what conclusions? What happens next?), descriptions of the user community and the library, a business review for the past year or so, or a glossary of technical terms. Write a one-page executive summary if the plan exceeds five pages. (This is a good format to distribute to your user community.)

To find samples of the plans of other libraries, try the Internet. These plans mostly come from large libraries, but you can get ideas from them. You can also ask around your town or city and among colleagues. Be sure to get a look at the plan of your parent organization. Your plan should follow its style.

The strategic plan should not be too detailed. If it is too specific it becomes outdated too soon. To write a good plan, the library must have underlying statistics. These will come from the statistics that you have kept throughout the year, past strategic plans, computer reports, or user surveys. Do not put in too much detail; if you think details will be requested, put them in an appendix or a separate document. Refer to the mission and objectives of the parent organization. Minimize library jargon. Use graphs or pictures instead of tables for the following: conclusions and supporting data; the mission, goals, objectives, and priorities; and the operating plan (implementation, action), time lines, results, and resources. Give the plan a title, perhaps taken from the vision or mission statement.

Here is a wonderful illustration by Daniel Baker, President of the American Concrete Institute, of how to categorize or describe a strategic plan and, more importantly, communicate it to the planners and users.

"To illustrate the meaning of *Strategy 2001* to ACI, we can create an acrostic out of the word STRATEGIC:

Specific—Our vision, purpose, and goals are clear and unambiguous;
Technical—Our focus is technical knowledge;
Relevant—We strive to meet the needs of the concrete industry;
Applicable—Our products are useful, practical, and beneficial;
Timely—Our technical knowledge is delivered in a timely manner;
Excellent—We strive to be the best in everything we do;
Growing—We grow by reaching an ever greater portion of the industry;
International—We think, work, and act with an international perspective; and
Concrete—What it's all about!"

The above combines many features of planning. Specific applies to the way the vision and mission statements and the goals are to be written; Technical to mission; Relevant to the users; Applicable to the outcomes; Timely to goals; Excellent to vision; Growing to goals; International to vision and users; and Concrete to vision." Baker added, "Strategic Planning is a never-ending and dynamic process. It begins with values and vision, and leads into purpose and mission."

Tailor the versions of the plan you send to staff, administration, and users to the needs and interests of the group. You probably will not send the same information to all. Write with your target audience in mind. Who are they? What do they expect? Should it be long or short, formal or informal? What is their experience or interest level? How much time do they have? When making oral presentations to senior management, Rae Cook (21) suggests stating your points out loud by saying: The point is . . . Do not be shy, indirect, or subtle. Provide specifics, interpretations, or conclusions for them. Use visual props, but keep them simple. Use simple graphs. Make only one point per visual prop. Use a headline with action verbs as a title for each one.

Cornerstone 4. Implement the Plan

Whew! You have finished the plan. Congratulate and reward yourself. But the hardest part is still before you—putting the plan into action. Long-range planning is cyclical. You write the plan, implement it, review and evaluate its success, decide what needs to be changed, and create a new plan incorporating the changes. "Someone once said as it relates to strategic planning, 'The genius is in the implementation.' By that is meant that the planning process itself is exciting and exhilarating while the follow up can be extremely tedious. However, it is the paying attention to the details and the deadlines that make the process work" (McCuistion).

Now is the time for tactical plans. "Tactics implement strategies" (Steiner, 176). Whereas strategic plans are for the future, tactical plans are for the present. The strategic provides the framework for the tactical. The tactical plan is where you create procedures and budgets and plan day-to-day activities. "Short-term, operational, or tactical plans encompass the day-to-day planning that takes place in any organization; this type of planning is more task-oriented. It involves a shorter time frame and the resolution of specific problems, usually of an internal nature" (Stueart and Moran, 38) (e.g., one-year's budget plans). "Because short-term plans are specific and immediate, they do not carry the uncertainty that strategic plans do" (Stueart and Moran, 39).

McKinsey & Co. has developed The Seven S framework for strategy implementation (Corrall, 36–37):

1. *Strategy:* plan of action
2. *Structure:* the way the library is organized
3. *Systems:* reports and routine processes and how information moves in the organization
4. *Staff:* how people are treated
5. *Style:* managerial style, corporate culture
6. *Skills:* what the library does well
7. *Shared values:* aspirations

It is extremely important to monitor the progress of your plan regularly. This includes evaluating the performance against your objectives. Reevaluate your priorities often. They can and do change. You should also do a full review a year or two before the end of the plan. Have a master to-do list of improvements to library service or reorganization that is categorized and prioritized according to library function. It will keep you focused and provide a road map of service initiatives. It also can be used as a communication or education tool when your boss wants to discuss goals or asks, "What do you do?"

Put project milestones and those of all members of your staff on your calendar. You may want to post a master calendar where everyone can see it (e.g., on the wall of a conference room) so that your staff members can see how their particular responsibilities fit into the whole picture. All staff members should be required to give periodic progress reports so that you, as manager, can locate and avoid problems before they become critical. (Quarterly is the minimum time period.) If someone gets behind, meet with the person immediately. Advise your supervisor about problems as they occur; management hates surprises. Do not assign blame. Acknowledge your responsibility, decide what must be done, and do it!

Why Strategic Planning May Fail

Sometimes, despite all your best intentions, a strategic plan—or part of it—may fail. It may be due to the process you used. Perhaps there was a failure to involve and gain the commitment of staff. The vision and mission may not have been closely linked to the goals of the parent institution.

It may be because of poor or unrealistic assumptions you made. You may have failed to account for organizational inertia. ("But we've always done it this way—we don't want to change.) Perhaps you underestimated the ability of politics to thwart the achievement of your objectives.

It may be because circumstances changed. The goals may have been overly ambitious—a common problem with first-time planners. The future may turn out different than expected. For example, resources were not made available, staff was cut, the economy took a downturn, or there was a change in management or ownership of the parent organization.

It may even be your fault. Perhaps you did not communicate the plan properly to management and your staff. Maybe you failed to follow through. Your work did not end with the writing of the plan. Did you continue to review and evaluate the progress of the plan? "Too much planning and not enough action can be just as bad as no planning at all" (Silber, 54).

You can minimize the likelihood of failure by avoiding the following mistakes. Take care that day-to-day, short-term planning does not become reactive, that is, finding solutions to problems only as they come up. Make sure that medium- and long-range projects do not get lost in the twin pressures of taking care of the routine and responding to crises. Additional planning traps are the following: thinking that planning will solve all ills, importing the successful plan of another library without making appropriate modifications, ignoring the corporate culture of the parent organization or the library, forgetting that planning is a learning process, not realizing that planning is also a political process, spending so much time on long-range planning that other managerial tasks are neglected, not being realistic in establishing goals, trying to do the plan in too short a time, or thinking the plan is cast in concrete.

Steiner (294) lists "Ten Major Mistakes to Avoid":

1. Assuming you can delegate it to a planner.
2. Being so involved in current crises [fire-fighting] that not enough time is spent on planning.
3. Failure to develop suitable goals. (These first three are very similar.)
4. Not involving line staff.
5. Not using plans to measure managerial performance.
6. Not creating a planning-friendly climate.
7. Separating planning from managing.
8. Making the process too formal.
9. Failure of top management to review the plans with the planning committee.
10. Top management not using the plan in decision-making.

What if all this does not work? You must give yourself permission to fail. As Stanley E. Smith (77) reminds us, "to reach any significant goal, you must leave your comfort zone." This applies not to your *physical* comfort zone but your *internal* one. You have learned and will do better the next time. Do not let one failed planning process keep you from trying it again. Planning is necessary to the ultimate success and continued existence of your library.

By using all the previous tips, I hope that you will be successful and not end up like this disillusioned librarian. A British high-tech corporate librarian says:

> I used to believe the trainers and the textbooks who told us that the solution to having too much to do in too little time was to PLAN!! Bitter experience has proved beyond any shadow of a doubt that planning, whether at home or at work, is a snare and a delusion, dreamed up by people who reckon that they can make a fast buck by writing books on telling people how to make plans!" [Present company not included, I hope.] The problem is that something always happens to throw any plan into disarray. The time spent on planning could have been far better spent on doing something useful, like one's job for example. The same goes for target setting. Either you reach your target, which to most people is a signal is to stop there and then, or, more probably, you don't—which simply makes you depressed, so you stop there and then.

Case Study

You are a solo librarian in a corporation. Develop a personal plan for professional development for submission to your boss. (This may include conferences, continuing education courses, memberships, and so on.) Include detailed benefits to you and your employer. Be as specific as possible.

5
Prioritization

One of the keys to time management is to focus each day's efforts on the activities that are truly important in realizing one's established goals.

J. Wesley Cochran, 21

Never confuse activity with results.

Lou Gerstner, CEO, IBM

Just because you *can* do something does not mean you *should.* This is a very difficult concept for most people, especially librarians. At the beginning of my management course for OPLs, I ask my students what they hope to get out of the course. When I started, the most common response was "I want to learn how to do it all." The short answer is: "You *don't* do it all." The long answer is this book.

But how do you decide which things to do and which to postpone or ignore? You have already learned how to do a strategic plan and determine your goals and objectives. You also have set up strategies for achieving these goals. Now you have to decide in which order you will implement these strategies. "Prioritizing is identifying the appropriate value and order of events" (Nutty).

Decision-Making

Most people agree that making decisions is hard. Why? You may not have enough information to make an informed choice. You may have too much information, and some of it may be conflicting or confusing.

You may have too many choices, several of which look equally attractive. Or you may have too few choices, none of which look good. Maybe there is not enough time for you to gather the information and make a decision you will feel good about. Or you know what you want to do but the resources you need are not available. Finally, you could just be making it a lot harder than necessary.

In Chapter 2 you learned about the Pareto 80/20 Principle. Koch (116–117) gives us five rules for decision-making using the 80/20 Principle:

1. "Not many decisions are very important." Twenty percent of decisions are important; the other 80 percent are not. The trick is to figure out the most important 20 percent. Don't agonize over the unimportant decisions, and don't overanalyze your decisions.
2. "The most important decisions often are those made only by default because turning points have come and gone without being recognized." Stay aware of what is going on around you so you do not miss that turning point and are involved in those important decisions.
3. "Gather 80 percent of the data and perform 80 percent of the relevant analyses in the first 20 percent of the time available, then make a decision 100 percent of the time and act decisively as if you were 100 percent confident that the decision is right." Once you have made the decision (to do or not to do), don't let yourself be pushed into changing your mind.
4. "If what you have decided isn't working, change your mind early rather than late." Cut your losses early, and abandon the project or task.
5. When something is working well, double and redouble your bets." Do not be wishy-washy. If it is working, stay with it.

There is no one right way to make a decision. We each have our own decision-making style. Tullier (139–140) identifies eight styles. The comments after each are my own.

1. *The Loner:* You make decisions on your own, with virtually no input from others. You run the risk of others thinking you are not a team player. Operating in a vacuum, you may not have all the necessary information or risk making a decision that does not mesh with other activities of the library or the parent organization.
2. *The Pollster:* You talk about your decision with and solicit input from "everyone." Although consensus-building is a great idea,

sometimes managers just have to take charge and make decisions on their own.

3. *The Forecaster:* When deciding, you put the focus on possible implications. Take care that you do not let the implications of your decision paralyze you and stop you from making a decision at all.

4. *The Bean-Counter:* You are very detail-oriented and collect as much information as possible. Do not spend so much time gathering data that you miss your critical decision point.

5. *The Analyst:* You spend a lot of time working out your options, sometimes instead of making a decision.

6. *The Feeler:* You often just go with your gut instinct. This is usually not a good idea, but when time is short sometimes it is absolutely necessary. An experienced manager is better able to be successful with this style.

7. *The Hunter-Gatherer:* You have to get "all" the information. There is no such thing as "all" the information. This is thinly disguised procrastination.

8. *The Settler:* You just want to get the process over with. Hasty decisions are often bad decisions. Do not rush the process. Make sure you have considered enough options.

How *should* you make a decision, then? First, ask how important is the decision? In other words, do you really even have to consider this issue? Then, are you ready to make the decision? Do you have enough information? What are your priorities? How does this question fit into them? What's your gut feeling about this? Do you think that it is a good idea or a bad one? Sometimes if you cannot shake the feeling that something is wrong, it is. Then, gather your information. Does this information change your priorities? Re-analyze the data, then listen to your gut again. Are there any barriers to making the decision? If not, decide!

"Simplify decision making by making routine decisions routine. When you have to make the same decision multiple times, you actually need a rule, not another decision" (Pollar, 44). When the same decision keeps coming up, create a procedure to handle it.

In any case, "Don't waste much time on trivial decisions" (Silber, 245). If one alternative is as good as the others, just pick one without a lot of deliberation or time spent. Go with your first instinct. "When in doubt, decide. Indecision is nearly always the worst mistake you can make. When tempted to postpone a decision, ask yourself: What will I know tomorrow that I do not know today? If the answer is nothing, just make the best decision you can and move ahead. In many cases, you will be able to adjust your course as you get more information"

(Hemphill, 14). "There are no bad decisions. Except no decision at all" (Silber, 108). "When you fail to make a decision it is usually made for you. Not to decide is to decide" (Clark and Clark, 132). Learn when to stop gathering information; you do not need *all* possible information to make a decision. To keep searching for data after enough is available to make the decision is a form of procrastination.

Once you decide, do not revisit the decision. "Today is the only day you can actually do anything" (Bruno, 8). You cannot re-live the past or control the future. Worrying if you made the right decision or second-guessing yourself accomplishes nothing and is a great time waster. Accept that you made the best decision you could based on the information available to you at the time. Just go on with life.

Step 1. Decide What to Do

"You don't really pay for things with money. You pay for them with time. And no matter what you do, you don't have enough time. That's just a fact of modern life. Which means you have to make choices" (Silber, 153). "You must organize your time so that you get done the things that must get done, you arrive at your meetings on time and prepared, you don't neglect your family or your life" (Silber, 23).

Prioritizing is based on your values, principles, vision, mission, promises made, and other people's priorities (or at least those that matter to you). Deciding what to do and what not to do is critical and requires continually checking your mission statement. Be aware that as you close in on your goals they may change. They may need to be upgraded or made more of a challenge. Each time something in your environment or job situation changes, you must reexamine the situation, your goals, and your priorities.

Prioritizing is often hard for librarians. Conventional library philosophy "discourages placing a higher value on one person's information needs than another's" (Cochran, 22). We seldom can do everything everyone wants us to do and should try to do so even less often. Besides, in the real world that we all live in, library users are not really created equal. There is always a hierarchy. Your boss's requests outrank those of one of your colleagues, an employee comes before a nonemployee, and often faculty get attention before students do. Also, some tasks are more important than are others. For instance, answering a reference question ranks higher than filing. You should be prepared for those with low-priority requests to complain because you are not acting on them. Discuss your priorities with your boss, and make sure that he or she will back up your decisions.

Without priorities you will choose the more enjoyable task, the task that takes the least time, the easier task, the familiar, or the task with a guaranteed good outcome. There is nothing wrong with this tendency; it is just human nature. But it is not the best way to determine what to do next. Prioritization also keeps you on the road to success, success as you have defined it for yourself. Be sure you are traveling on the right road, that you are going where you *want* to go, that you enjoy—or, better, *love*—what you're doing.

Clark suggests dividing potential projects or tasks into three categories: those that will succeed without you, those that will fail no matter what you do, and those in which you can make a difference. Put your efforts where they will do the most good—in the last category. In a complex, multipart project, "decide which tasks are critical and must be completed" on schedule and "how long non-critical tasks can be delayed before they affect your ability to meet the deadline" (Allen, 25).

	Important	Not Important
Urgent	1	Should be 3 Usually is 2
Not Urgent	Should be 2 Usually is 3	Should be 4; often moves ahead of others

Figure 5.1. Prioritization or Decision-Making Matrix.

Another way to prioritize is to realize that every task is either important or not important and urgent or not urgent (see the decision matrix in Figure 5.1). If it is important *and* urgent, then it should be your first priority. If it is important but not urgent, it should be your second priority. However, because people tend to react faster to urgent questions than to important ones, these issues are often pushed back to priority three. Your third priority should be items that are urgent, but not important. The lowest priority, number four, should be whatever is neither urgent nor important. Unfortunately, these routine tasks are too often taken out of turn simply because they tend to pile up (e.g., re-shelving books, opening mail, or retrieving voice or e-mail messages) or are easier or more interesting than the more important projects.

"Progress means moving resources from low-value to high-value uses" (Koch, 126). Koch (161–162) goes on to list the top 10 low- and high-value uses of time. I do not agree with all of them—see my comments in brackets—but they can give you a good idea of how to use your own time.

The top 10 low-value uses of time follow:

1. Things other people want you to do. [Yes, but most reference questions are of this type. One of the strong suits of librarians is our ability and willingness to make others' questions our own.]
2. Things that have always been done this way.
3. Things you are not unusually good at doing. [Outsource or delegate these tasks.]
4. Things you do not enjoy doing. [You will probably not do a particularly good job.]
5. Things that are always interrupted. [Unfortunately, nearly everything we do falls into this category—especially for OPLs.]
6. Things few other people are interested in.
7. Things that have already taken twice as long as you had originally expected. [Do you really want to put more time into this time sink?]
8. Things where your collaborators are unreliable or of low quality.
9. Things that have a predictable cycle. [Finding a way to do these tasks easier the next time is a good idea and a good use of your time now.]
10. Answering the telephone. [Answering the telephone every time it rings *is* a low-value use of time. Answering it at specific times is *not.*]

The top 10 highest-value uses of time:

1. Things that advance your overall purpose in life. [Or things that advance your work goals.]
2. Things you have always wanted to do. [*If* you have the time, ability, and approval from your boss and *if* they fit into your strategic plan.]
3. Things already in the 80/20 relationships of time to results.
4. Innovative ways of doing things that promise to slash the time required and/or multiply the quality of results. [These are the things

that you come up with by quiet thinking, instead of working all the time!]

5. Things other people tell you cannot be done. [If you accomplish them you look like a hero, but be sure the upside potential exceeds the down side.]
6. Things that other people have done successfully in a different arena. [These, like number four, can save you valuable time down the road.]
7. Things that use your own creativity. [You will be more likely to enjoy the task at hand.]
8. Things that you can get other people to do for you with relatively little effort on your part. [Yes! Delegation is a good idea, but make sure that you do not delegate the strategic core of your job.]
9. Anything with high-quality collaborators who have already transcended the 80/20 rule of time, who use time eccentrically and effectively.
10. Things for which it is now or never. [Unfortunately, the urgent project sometimes must take priority.]

Winston (132) suggests a payoff dichotomy for prioritizing. High-payoff tasks may be high risk or take time to see results. They can be easy to put off because they take time and are not "urgent." Because these tasks are the ones that will most improve your image or value in the organization, try to work on at least one every day. Negative-payoff tasks are must-dos because delaying or ignoring them can hurt you, your image, or the organization. These include important paperwork (especially of the legal variety), true emergencies, or direct requests by your boss—or your boss's boss. Weeks (46–48) describes high-priority tasks as the ones that are most crucial to management, take the most time, or involve others. They are why you were hired. Besides, by doing them first you can avoid creating work stress for yourself. "Projects with the highest monetary impact and/or the highest visibility take priority." A Canadian business librarian is very realistic. "Requests from high profile clients or clients who have been vocally supportive of the library tend to get the higher priority. It's not necessarily fair, but image is part of survival and they contribute to the library image, so are more important from a strategic perspective."

Do high-priority or high-payoff tasks when you are most alert and at your best. Save the medium-payoff tasks—the day-to-day or routine—for low-energy times (right after lunch, at the end of the day). What about the low-payoff tasks? Avoid, delegate, or ignore them. These include creating reports no one reads, micromanaging others, most surfing of the Internet, and overanalyzing statistics.

Question Everything

Asking why or why not is key to prioritization. Corcoran (19) suggests asking three questions about each task that comes your way:

1. Is it necessary? Should it even be done at all?
2. Do you have to do it, or is this something anyone could do? Do you add value?
3. Is there a better way to do it? My mantra as a librarian is "better, cheaper, faster." Being inherently lazy, I am always trying to find an easier way to accomplish whatever I need to do.

When someone brings you an emergency, ask, "Is this really a crisis? Is it really *my* crisis?" We have all seen the sign that says, "Failure to plan on *your* part does not constitute an emergency on *my* part," but do you really implement this idea? When a client always leaves things to the last minute and brings you information requests that you cannot possibly fulfill properly in the time allowed, do you tell the client the truth or just do your best (which is never really your best)? A Canadian business librarian says:

> Don't just accept a client's claim that they need information by a particular date or time. Question and negotiate. The client may not need *all* information by their stated deadline. You may be able to provide the specific information that is needed with additional non-urgent information following later, thus allowing you to meet multiple deadlines and keep several people happy.

I suggest doing whatever you can for the client—the first time only. Tell the client that this is just a one-time response. In the future, if he or she brings you a request with an impossible deadline you will decline it (politely but firmly). This should result in changed behavior. If it does not, you have made your policy clear. (Make sure your boss agrees with you and will back you up on this.)

Another tactic for dealing with emergencies is to determine if the emergency is real or imagined—or perhaps even manufactured. Can the task be postponed without irreparable harm to you or the institution? Is it the best use of your time to deal with it now? (After dealing with the emergency, be sure you get back to the task you were doing before the interruption. Figure out what you need to do to catch up, regroup, or minimize damage to your schedule.)

Sometimes you can ignore a request until the requestor asks again. This is the "squeaky wheel" approach (Aslett, 33). I found that this was the only way to deal with one of my bosses. He would ask me for something, then not respond when I did it. Later, I was told by one of his other subordinates that you should not even start something until he had asked for the third time. Once I started following that advice I found I had much more time for projects my boss *really* thought were important.

"If someone else drops the ball, do you really have to pick it up?" (Mackenzie, 91). In being helpful we often will offer to take on a task that someone else started but either failed to complete or did not complete satisfactorily. It is probably all right to do this every now and then—if you have the time and interest and if it fits into your long-term plans. However, you do not want to become the person everyone counts on to finish what others do not want to do. Resist temptation, and force yourself to just say no!

Other questions to ask include the following. How will I know if I am successful? How will I be rewarded? If these are not clear, you should consider turning down the job. It is not selfish, only prudent, to ask: What's in it for me? or What's the payoff going to be?

Will the task require more time than it is worth? If it is a good project, can it be downsized, simplified, or streamlined? Can you get someone to help on it? Can you extend the deadline?

Will doing it make me bored, unhappy, or even miserable? If so, turn it down. You will do a good job on the project, and this is not a good thing.

What have I got to lose? Are the consequences of failure smaller (and not disastrous) than the rewards of success?

What will I have to give up? Look at this in terms of your time. What other tasks could you do if you do not accept this project (This is called the *opportunity cost*.) If you can live with the answer, go ahead and do the project. On the reverse side, ask: What will I really be missing out on or losing if I turn this down? Again, can you live with the answer?

What is the objective? If you do not know why you are doing a task, it is very hard to do it well. If the requestor cannot explain the objective to you, then something is really wrong.

And, finally, this trio. Should it even be done at all? Is this trip necessary? (My mother's favorite phrase.) And my favorite, will the world come to an end if. . . ? (I haven't had a positive answer to this one yet.)

QUESTION:
Your boss adds a rush project to your schedule, which is already more than full. What do you do?

ANSWER:
Eisenberg (62) suggests you accept the job, but make a list of your current priorities and ask for a meeting with your boss to discuss them. According to St. James (144), you can ask which of your other tasks can you *not* do to get this project done.

Step 2. Decide When to Do It

Now that you know what you are going to do (and not do), you have to decide when to do each task. Some tasks need to be done right now, some need to be done today, some tomorrow, and some can be put in the "whenever there is time" category. Bond (9) tells of one manager who made a sign for himself that said, "I must do the most productive thing possible at every given moment" and looked at it whenever he got distracted. This seems very compulsive and unrealistic to me. You occasionally have to relax, think, goof off, or listen to others. Overschedule yourself and you will burn out.

I like the guiding principle suggested by Alan Lakein (in Cochran, 29). "What is the best use of my time *right now*?" Ask yourself this question several times a day or whenever there is any question about what to do next. What was important a few hours ago may not be right for now. Make sure the things you are working on are still needed. This is especially true if you are going to set aside a time to be undisturbed. Be sure you use it to work on the highest-priority task or tasks.

You can also apply the 80/20 rule to reaching your goals. "You can be eighty percent effective by achieving twenty percent of your goals [or] successfully completing only the two most important items on your list" (LeBoeuf, 41). Prioritizing and planning ensure that you are doing the right 20 percent.

Some tasks lend themselves to what McGee-Cooper (202) calls "natural prioritizing or executive neglect": If you ignore them, they might just go away. Determine what does *not* need to be done and don't do it. Reevaluate routine tasks to see what can be done more efficiently or what can be left undone. Spend time developing long-term reusable solutions that will make things easier in the future. Allow subordinates to make (or ask your boss to let you make) decisions on an exception basis. This is when you act as you see fit, unless told otherwise. Do tasks adequately rather than thoroughly.

De Stricker (32) applies the suggestions above to libraries:

> The bottom line for us all is this: Are we participating in the knowledge management activities that will ensure our organization's continued success, or are we running an information center? What library school rules can be ignored in favor of strategic work (such as meeting with key stakeholders one-on-one)? Where can we cut corners so we can focus on our vision for the next five years?

You have to be realistic. You cannot expect to be involved in strategic, important, and exciting projects every minute of every day. "A typical librarian manager may spend a significant portion of every day in non-managerial activities" (Cochran, 12). This is not altogether bad. This keeps you grounded in what is going on in the trenches. As an OPL, you will *have* to do boring, routine, or seemingly unimportant tasks because there is no one else to do them. Dusting the shelves or filing or alphabetizing circulation cards is as much a part of the job of being a librarian as reference or research or online searching. To be a professional is to do what is necessary for the smooth running of your library and to provide high-quality service to your clients as competently as possible, whether or not the tasks are "professional tasks."

Step 3. Decide How to Do It

Perfectionism is the enemy of time management, prioritization, efficiency, and effectiveness. According to Eisenberg (224) perfectionists "give every task the same value." They are indecisive, always waiting for the perfect answer, tool, or time. They often start a task but don't finish it, or they take too long doing it because it is never perfected. Finally, perfectionists tend to need to do everything themselves. To minimize this self-destructive behavior, try the following. "Accept that others know more than you about some things" (Pollar, 7). You are not always the right person to do a job (or make a decision). Let go. Keep things in perspective, and realize when perfection is not required. (A hint—it seldom is.) Know when to quit. Focus on results. As long as the task is completed, it does not matter if the process is imperfect. Don't be so hard on yourself. You often learn the most from your mistakes. In *Managing Our Frantic Lives* (1994, in Silber, 235), Natasha Josefowitz writes "Losing Battles":

> By trying to be
> Everywhere at once
> I am nowhere
> By trying to be
> Everyone to too many
> I am no one.

You Can—and Should—Say No!

"No!—the Greatest Time-Saver of All Time" (Silber, 235). You have decided what you should do, and when and how to do it. Now you just have to learn how to say no to anything that does not fit in. But saying no is one of the hardest things for most librarians to do. We all want to help people—that was a major reason we chose this profession. We are afraid that if we say no to a client, he or she will not like us.

Why are we afraid to say no? We are often driven by a desire to win the approval of others or by a false sense of obligation. We simply do not know how to say no or haven't the time to think of a better answer. If your objectives and priorities are not clear to you and your clients, the thoughtless assumption by others is that you will say yes. Perhaps you feel you just cannot say no to your boss. We all want to be liked, to win the approval of others. We also may feel that it is our obligation to do whatever others ask of us. We may be rushed into a response, and it is usually easier to say yes than no.

If you don't say no, what happens? You feel overwhelmed, tired, or stressed. You feel victimized and resentful. You try to do everything and, as a consequence, either do nothing or do nothing well. Bernard Meltzer sums it up this way. "I cannot give you a formula for success. But I can give you the formula for failure. It's this: Try to please everyone" (McGee-Cooper, 203).

Why don't you say no?

- You may have lost sight of your priorities. You have been taught that "good little girls and boys don't say no" (McGee-Cooper, 189).
- You want to please everyone. Forget it; you can't please everyone. Decide whom it is important to please—your boss, yourself.
- You do not want to hurt anyone's feelings; this is closely related to wanting to please everyone. Remember, the person who asked you

to do something that you should not be doing is not thinking about *your* feelings.

- You don't think you can say no to your boss, or you are afraid you will lose your job. There are very few situations in which a no response will cause your boss to fire you. Bosses are notorious for asking us to do things that we should not do, either because they do not want to do the task themselves or because they think you will say yes because you are afraid not to.
- You suffer from low self-esteem; you do not think that your priorities are as important as are those of others.
- Ego. This is the reverse of low self-esteem; you think your priorities are the most important.
- You believe that the customer is always right. Yes, the customer is important, but he or she is not always right; you need to be able to recognize these times.
- You are too curious; you say yes because the project is interesting, not because it is important.
- You do not want to be left out, or you want to be seen as a team player. Working as a team is important, but getting your own work done is more important. Ultimately you are judged on your own work.
- You really think you can do it; you have not consulted your schedule or are overly optimistic about the time or resource requirements of the project.
- You are afraid that you will miss a great opportunity. If it's really a great opportunity, you are going to have to say no to something else. Perhaps it is time to reevaluate your priorities.
- You are honored to be asked; thank the person for the honor, but politely decline the "honor." "Beware of playing roles in life that you think you *should* have; instead, take on only those responsibilities that mean something to you (Tullier, 37).
- You want to keep busy. If you are bored or underscheduled, you need to talk with your boss about adding some duties. If this is a temporary situation, be especially careful about saying yes to a new responsibility. It may become yours permanently—even when you *do not* have time. This is called *expectation creep*.
- You don't take time to think it over; it is much easier and quicker to say yes than to think of a good reason to say no. Also say no to negative people or those whom you can never please.

The following comment was written about accountants, but it reads just as true when you substitute "librarian" for "CPA." "Most CPAs are jealous entrepreneurs. They built their practices [or reputations] based on personal service to their clients and are understandably reluctant to do anything that might jeopardize that personal service relationship" (Ainsworth, 19). You can and must get over this reluctance.

How to Say No

As good librarians, obsessed with quality customer service, our first inclination is to say yes to every request that comes along, whether it is from a customer or the boss. But you simply cannot do everything for everyone. Sometimes the answer must be no.

Say no when the request is clearly out of your scope. (You do have a written mission statement, don't you?) I was never afraid to tell a client that he or she should try the public library when I did not have the resources to answer the question or was asked to find the answer to a child's homework question. Say no when someone else can answer the question better or less expensively. This could be another library, another department in the organization, or an information broker. Say no when asked to do something illegal or unethical. This could be copying an entire book, ordering something on the company account for personal use, or industrial espionage. You simply tell the requestor that the request is illegal or unethical and your personal and professional code of ethics will not permit you to fill it. You should also say no if doing something will just make you feel uncomfortable. Say no when you really do not want to do the job. This is a close call, especially when it comes to your boss; however, you should never do something you really do not want to do. Sometimes you might have to decide between doing something you do not want to and finding another job. This is another issue, but it does come up and you should be prepared to address it.

But how should you say no? Not knowing how to refuse a request frequently is a problem for librarians. Saying no firmly and gracefully is an art you can learn. Realize first that you cannot say yes to everything or meet everyone's requests for your time without sacrificing your own (Turner). Never say yes without thinking about it first. Don't just say no; offer a counterproposal, an alternative. Never make a promise you cannot keep. Keep your goals and priorities in mind. If this project does not advance them, say no. "Don't say: 'I'm sorry'—it weakens your 'no.' Make a simple explanation—a long-winded one weakens your 'no.' If you sense a request coming [that you do not want to do], be proactive and say 'no' first. Once you have said 'no,' stick with it. Rehearse and practice how to say 'no.' Do not let your body language defeat you (looking away, speaking softly or too slowly)." It is your library and your responsibility. You have the right to set policy. Be firm.

Saying no is difficult. When you are getting ready to speak out—or say no—first figure out what is the worst that can happen. Is it worth it? Can you live with it?

To make things easier when you are overcommitted, St. James suggests saying no to all commitments for the next month. When you say no to all, no one can feel slighted and it lowers the stress on you because you do not have to decide.

There are several kinds of no according to an article in *Arthritis Today*. The sweet-talk no: sugarcoat it, but say no nevertheless. The bait-and-switch no: suggest something else in its place, but still say no. The to-the-point no: just say no. The explanatory no: give a reason—a reason, not an excuse—then say no. And finally, the silent no: the one you say to yourself. "It's always smart to say 'no' when it allows you to say 'yes' to something you really want to do" (Smart, 47). Note that the ultimate result of each of these statements is *no*. No matter how you say it, be sure your message comes through loud and clear.

Saunders (9–11) suggests these seven steps to help you become more assertive and be able to say no:

1. "Commit yourself to changing your behavior."
2. "Learn to value yourself."
3. "Develop an action plan."
4. "When faced with a decision, focus on the business implications of your answer"—concentrate on that, not on your fears.
5. "'No' should be the first word out of your mouth if it is the better answer." Don't weaken it with apologies.
6. "Don't wait to be asked something to say 'no.'" Take the initiative.
7. "Rehearse difficult conversations." Try role-playing with a friend or colleague (perhaps even one who also has trouble saying no).

Be quick and decisive. "Do not raise false hopes through indecision." "Say no rapidly before people can anticipate that you may say yes" (LeBoeuf, 79).

Be polite. Say that you would really like to say yes, but you are overcommitted, or it just does not fit into your plans right now, or whatever other polite turn-down is appropriate.

Because it is very hard to get out of a commitment or reduce its limits once you have said yes and is not a good idea even if you can, say no if there is any question of whether you can handle the task. Remember that you do not want to create an unhappy customer.

Never say yes without thinking it over first. Suggested replies:

- "Can I get back to you on that?"
- "I have to check my schedule. I'll call you tomorrow."
- Or, if all else fails, "I have to check with my boss." Then ask him or her for help in framing your negative reply.

Do not say "maybe." It's wishy-washy. You are partly committing yourself when you say, "Maybe next time." Is that what you mean to do? Just say no.

"Learn to say no *without guilt.* Saying no without guilt is not selfish—it's a protective necessity" (Carlson, 215, 216). Everyone says no once in a while, so there is no need to feel bad about doing it.

When you have to say no to your boss, Mackenzie (126) suggests that you "remind him or her of your other projects...and ask for help in deciding where the new assignment should fall on the list of priorities."

Step 4. Reevaluating Your Priorities

Berner (in Siess) says:

> Priorities are not constant. While it is helpful to list tasks and goals in writing and to assign them a priority, you cannot make the mistake of thinking that they are carved in stone. Priorities are constantly shifting as new tasks and new developments come into play. Whatever you may be working on, for example, it is likely that if your boss calls or comes in with a request, that request is going to become your number one priority (unless, of course, your boss's boss calls with a request, and then you may have to reevaluate). The important thing is to recognize that whatever criteria you may use for determining priority— and there are many—you should always be working on your highest priority items at any given time.

But remember that you should strive to be doing the highest-priority task for that time, not just the highest-priority task.

Here are more tips for prioritization:

- You don't have to do everything everybody tells you to do.
- Learn the difference between what you *should* do and what you *need* to do.
- You don't have to do everything the way other people tell you to do it.

- You don't have to do everything according to someone else's time frame.
- You don't always have to do everything yourself.
- Yes, you have to please other people, but you also have to please yourself.

Librarians on Priorities

- "Stop every now and then and think, 'Am I wasting time here, or am I using it productively?' For example, the Internet gives many opportunities for doing the latter, but also many temptations for straying off the straight and narrow (to check the latest from Wimbledon, for example). By setting 'stop and think' points at 30-minute intervals during the day, you can drag yourself back to what you *should* be doing!" (a British high-tech corporate librarian).
- "I've hired a coach. She helps me focus and prioritize. What works for me one week or one month may change. Realizing this was a big help. I was using a regular Day Timer®. Now I set out a pile of manageable stuff to get through in one day. I am also starting to use the Task section of Microsoft Outlook®" (an independent information broker).
- "When I'm really into whatever I am doing, and think of something else I must do, I write it down, and eventually have a to-do list, and then start work on those things the next day, or whenever it seems appropriate. It is not a priority list, but I do set priorities if the list has five or more items" (a librarian in an information research firm).
- "Constantly ask yourself: Does this have to be done? Is there an easier way? In a solo library things don't have to be done by the book, so to speak, although you do need to consider whether someone taking over your position can easily figure out what you've done" (a corporate librarian).
- "Customers expect me to be at my desk. At the same time, department managers expect me to do outreach activities with business units that take me away from my desk. I haven't resolved this, except to message my contrasting objectives to all parties and let them know I do my best to be both places at once" (a corporate librarian).
- "As part of our performance review process, all employees are required to set objectives on at least a semi-annual basis, so this

forces me to think strategically. I try to decide what's important by first looking at my department—what are my manager's goals and objectives and how can I help? Then I look to my customers' goals. These are often inter-related, so it's not difficult. Lastly, I look at my own professional development or skills I need. I use my managers' priorities as guidelines for what's important when thinking strategically and conducting business planning. In terms of the day to day, though, I prioritize rather loosely. Sometimes I use first-in, first-out, but rarely is it that simple. If I can answer someone's question in five minutes, I'm apt to break away from what I'm doing to do that so that they can move on. With so much to do, though, I tend to think, 'What would my manager want me to focus on?' I will also negotiate with a customer who has more than one request in at a time—'I can work on this now,' I might say, 'but that would mean putting off for a day or two the other project you asked me about.' And I let them decide. I will also set time line boundaries with customers when they have research projects when possible. Sometimes I don't have a chance to do that—they might need something immediately. But I try to explain that a project will take me a certain amount of time and why; this helps set their expectations" (a corporate librarian).

- "Try to fill the personal request for information above every other duty. Cataloging, filing and routine library maintenance take second place to fulfilling the personal request for information. At some point, however, the routine duties must be kept up to enable you to fulfill the information request! Obviously, it's a balancing act" (a corporate librarian).
- "I have discovered that customers are often most impressed by the things that take the least time, and do not appreciate the effort that goes into some of our most time-consuming duties. We need to keep that in mind when setting our priorities" (an American librarian).
- [In a position downsized from 40 to 16 hours] "My solution was deciding that filing the journals as they returned from circulation was the task to do last on the list, consequently this task was never done. I have a reputation as a hard worker in the organisation, so people knew it wasn't laziness that caused the lack of filing. I ended the problem by doing a time management course that was being offered within the organisation to "prove" that there was simply not enough time to complete all tasks necessary to do my job satisfactorily. This then gave me the ammunition to go to the VP and say that I needed to increase my hours. Result—4 extra hours per week. I can do the job in the 20 hours per week I now

work. (Although filing returned journals is still at the bottom of the to-do list!)" (an Australian corporate librarian).

Case Studies

You work in a solo library in a corporation. You are given an unlimited budget for technology. Develop a two-year *prioritized* plan for technology acquisition. Explain why each item was chosen and the reason for the order of acquisition.

You are an OPL in a government hospital. However, you have always had clerical support (most recently, two full-time equivalents). Now you are told that your support staff has been reassigned to another department, and you are now a *true* solo. Without help, how can you continue the high level of service that you have been providing to your clientele? Or can you?

ANSWER: You *can't* continue all the services you used to provide. You should go to your boss and ask, "Now that I have only one-third of the resources that I used to have, which one-third of the library services do you want me to discontinue?" Suggest outsourcing those vital services that you no longer have time to provide (e.g., document delivery or cataloging). Ask if you can "borrow" one of your former associates when things pile up or for special projects. If there is a library school in your vicinity, see if you can hire an intern to help out or host a practicum student (to whom no stipend is paid). (Remember, however, that it will take time to supervise an intern or student.) If your organization uses volunteers, perhaps you can have one or more assigned to the library.

Never, repeat, *never* say to your boss, "I'll manage." This just tells him or her that you didn't really need the help in the first place and will make it nearly impossible to regain those two lost positions.

Appendix A
Additional Resources

Books

Asantewa, D. (1992). *Strategic Planning for Special Libraries*. Washington, D.C.: Special Libraries Association, ISBN 0-8711-1399-6. Dated and mainly for larger libraries, but has a good sample plan.

Drucker, Peter F. (1973). *Management: Task, Responsibilities, Practices*. New York, N.Y.: Harper and Row, ISBN 0-06011-092-9.

Foster, Charles. (2001). *What Do I Do Now? Dr Foster's 30 Laws of Great Decision Making*. New York, N.Y.: Simon and Schuster, ISBN 0-68486-919-5.

Gallagher, Winifred. (1994). *The Power of Place: How Our Surroundings Shape Our Thoughts, Emotions, and Actions*. New York, N.Y.: Harper, ISBN 0-0609-7602-0.

Giescke, Joan, ed. (1998). *Scenario Planning for Libraries*. Chicago, Ill.: American Library Association, ISBN 0-8389-3482-X. From material originally presented at a conference entitled, "Transforming Libraries: A National Conference and Exhibition on Leadership and Technology in the Technology Age," 1996.

Goodstein, Leonard D. (1985). *Understanding Applied Strategic Planning: A Manager's Guide*. San Diego, Calif.: University Associates, ISBN 0-88390-183-8.

Hoch, Stephen L., Howard C. Kunreuther, and Stephen J. Hoch. (2001). *Wharton on Making Decisions*. New York, N.Y.: John Wiley, ISBN 0-47138-247-7.

Houk, Margaret. (1996). *Lighten Up and Enjoy Life More: Everyday Ways to De-Stress Your Lifestyle*. Valley Forge, Pa.: Judson Press,

ISBN 0-8170-1240-0. The content is directed more toward women, and the book is written from a Christian viewpoint.

Kaplan, Robert S., and David P. Norton. (2000). *The Strategy-Focused Organization.* Cambridge, Mass.: Harvard Business School Publishing, ISBN 1-57851-250-6.

Lakein, Alan. (1974). *How to Get Control of Your Time and Your Life.* New York, N.Y.: Dutton, ISBN 0-45116772-4.

Levy, Lois. (1999). *Undress Your Stress: 30 Curiously Fun Ways to Take Off Tension.* Naperville, Ill.: Sourcebooks, ISBN 1-57071-482-7.

Nelson, Sandra, Ellen Altman, and Diane Mayo. (2000). *Managing for Results: Effective Resource Allocation for Public Libraries.* Chicago, Ill.: American Library Association, ISBN 0-83893-498-6.

Seiwert, Lother J. (1991). *Time is Money: Save It.* New York, N.Y.: Kogan Page, ISBN 0-74940-460-4.

Simon, Herbert A. (1966). *The Shape of Automation for Men and Management: The New Science of Management Decision,* 2nd ed. New York, N.Y.: Harper and Row.

Taylor, Bernard, and John R. Sparkes, eds. (1997). *Corporate Strategy and Planning.* New York, N.Y.: Halstead Press, ISBN 0-47098-035-1.

Taylor, Harold. (1981). *Making Time Work for You: A Guidebook to Effective and Productive Time Management.* New York, N.Y.: Beaufort Books, ISBN 0-82530-064-9.

Wilson, Paul. (1999). *Calm at Work.* New York, N.Y.: Plume, ISBN 0-45228-042-7.

Articles

Alonzo, Vincent. (1998). "Planning Success—One Day at a Time." *Incentive,* October, 172(10):123–124. Interview with Hyrum W. Smith, Chairman of Franklin Covey Co.

Biasella, Tina. (2001). "Practice What You Preach," *SBN Cleveland,* November, p. 31.

Blohowiak, Don. (1998). "Getting the Work Done." *Association Management,* December, 50(13):23.

Boyd, Ernest. (2000). "Setting Priorities." *Association Management,* February, 52(2):131.

Cone, Lois M. (2001). "Seven Habits of Highly Effective Librarians." *Church and Synagogue Librarians,* March-April, 34(5):10.

DeGennaro, Richard. (1978). "Library Administration and New Management Systems." *Library Journal,* 15 December, 103(22):2480.

Denton, Stephanie. (2001). "Don't Read This Article Now. You Can Do It Later." *The Small Business Journal.* *http://www.tsbj. com/editorial/02120610.htm*; accessed 9 April. The author is a board member of the National Association of Professional Organizers.

Edwards, Gary. (2001). "Managing Up: Taking Responsibility for the Relationship with Your Boss," *http://ihavegoals.com/public/ articles*; accessed 10 July.

Epstein, Marc J., and Robert A. Westbrook. (2001). "Linking Actions to Profits in Strategic Decision Making." *MIT Sloan Management Review*, Spring, 40(3):39–49.

George, Paul. (2001). "Care and Maintenance of the Successful Career: How Experienced Law Librarians Make Their Work Rewarding." *Law Library Journal*, Fall, 93(4): 535-587.

Glieck, James. (1999). "How Much Time...Can a Person Devote to Timesaving?" *Across the Board*, November, 36(10): 9–10.

_____. (2000). Past as Prologue." *OLA Quarterly*, [Oregon Library Association], Fall, 6(3):4–11.

Hayes, Suzi. (1998). "Strategic Planning Web Sites." *Information Outlook*, February, 2(2):12–13.

Hulser, Richard P. (1998). "Integrating Technology in Strategic Planning." *Information Outlook*, February, 2(2):24–27.

Kaplan, Robert S., and David P. Norton. (2000). "Having Trouble with Your Strategy? Then Map It." *Harvard Business Review*, September, 78(5):167–171.

Morgan, Nick. (2001). "Put Your Decision Making to the Test: Communicate." *Harvard Management Communication Letter*, November, 4(11):1–3.

Peterson, Lisa C. (1997). "Time Management for Library Professionals." *Katherine Sharp Review*, Winter, No. 5, *http://www.lis. uiuc.edu/review/5/Peterson.html*; accessed 4 April 2001.

Powe, Kathleen Begley, and Daniel Plung. (2001). "Strategic Decision Making in a Time of Information Overload." *Information Outlook*, November, 5(11):22–30.

Proudfit, Chuck. (2001). "Strategic Planning: Failing to Plan is Planning to Fail." *The Small Business Journal, http://www.tsbj. com/editorial/02060803.htm*; accessed 20 May.

Reynolds, Katie, (2001). "Retooling Yourself for Work in the 21st Century," presentation at the Annual Meeting of the AALL.

Robinson, Cathy, *et al.* (1998). "Arlington County (Virginia) Public Libraries Look to the Future." In *Scenario Planning for Libraries,* Joan Giesecke, ed., pp. 47–78. Chicago, Ill.: American Library Association, ISBN 0-8389-3482-X.

Spring, Kathy. (2001). "Out of Order (Judith Tapiero). Freelance Corporate Librarian." *1099*, *http://1099.com/c/ar/di/librarian_d024. html*; accessed 8 May.

Williams, Charli. (1996). "Focusing on Results...Why Time Management Doesn't Work." (Part 1). *Broker World*, August, pp. 106–108.

——. (1996). "Focusing on Results...Why Time Management Doesn't Work." (Part 2). *Broker World*, September, pp. 118–120.

Yamauchi, Kent T. (2001). "Procrastination: Ten Ways to 'Do It Now.'" Virginia Polytechnic Institute and University, Division of Student Affairs, Cook Counseling Center, *http://www.ucc.vt. edu/stdysk/procrast.html;* accessed 26 March.

Zbar, Jeffery D. (2000). "Home Office Simplified." *Home Office Computing*, July, 18(7):54–58.

Journal

The Informed Librarian: Professional Reading for the Information Professionals. Infosources Publishing (Arlene Eis), 140 Norma Road, Teaneck, N.J. 07666. U.S.$99/year, monthly. Contains a table of contents and current awareness tool for librarians. Subscribing is a great way to keep up without the expense of subscribing to lots of journals. A photocopy service is available at a very reasonable cost.

Websites

123 Sort It (2001). At *http://www.123sortit.com*; accessed 30 April. Contains lots of good tips on self-management, project management, voice mail, e-mail, snail mail, desktop management, paper files, interruptions, and more.

Business.com (2001). At *http://www.business.com*; accessed 20 May. Lists of Web sites, white papers, and articles on management and strategic planning.

Childress, Karen. (2001). "Making Decisions Effectively" at *http://ihavegoals.com/public/articles*; accessed 10 July.

Ihavegoals.com. (2001). At *http://ihavegoals.com*; accessed 10 July. A brand-new site (1 March 2001), this has information on goal-setting, goals and organization quizzes, and an article archive. If you join (U.S.$12.95 per month), you get a coach who is supposed to help you create and reach your personal and professional goals.

Organizations

Alliance for Nonprofit Management, 1899 L Street, NW, 6th Floor, Washington, D.C. 20036. Phone: 1-202-955-8406; Fax: 1-202-955-8419; e-mail: alliance@allianceonline.org; Web site: *http:// www.allianceonline.org*; accessed 20 May 2001. Look at their strategic planning FAQ.

National Association of Professional Organizers, P.O. Box 140647, Austin, Tex. 78714. Phone: 1-512-206-0151; Fax: 1-512-454-3036; Web site: *http://www.napo.net*. A nonprofit organization founded in 1985. Now has over 1,200 members, including consultants, speakers, trainers, authors; and has manufacturing products.

Videos

But I Don't Have Customers. 21 minutes, 1994. The accompanying book has agendas for one-, two-, and four-hour training sessions, pre- and post-tests, overheads, and so on. American Media Incorporated, 4900 University Avenue, West Des Moines, Iowa 50206-6769. Phone: 1-515-224-0256 or 1-800-262-2557. Purpose: "to help your employees understand the importance of each other and the roles that they play in your organization." Very good at what it does, this book also is easy to understand. Shows a corporate situation, but is easily translated to a library.

The 59-Second Mind Map: Unstick Your Priorities for Greater Productivity. 27 minutes, 1995. Comes with a handout, two audiotapes, and a book, $295.00 Sound Communication, 1388 Alki Avenue, SW, Seattle, Wash. 98116. Phone 1-206-935-0887; e-mail: rkonieczka@aol.com. Book alone is $9.95 from Hara Publishing, P.O. Box 19732, Seattle, Wash. 98109. ISBN 1-883697-38-7. Dr. Richard Konieczka, a former mechanical engineer, MBA, and investment advisor and now a lecturer, goes through his Mind Map process of organizing thought and priorities. Light and easy, a bit too much detail on what is essentially a very simple process.

Appendix B
Forms

Time-Waster Form

Date	Time Waster	Solution	Notes

Adapted from Bond, 34.

Appendix B

Worksheet for Procrastination-Ending Action Plan

Task	Easy Step	Start	Finish
1.			
2.			
3.			
4.			
5.			
6.			
7.			
8.			
9.			
10.			
11.			
12.			
13.			
14.			
15.			

Adapted from Clark.

Analyzing Interruptions

Priority	What?	Why?	How Long?	How to Eliminate?

Adapted from Ferner, 144.

Delegation Worksheet

Task to be Performed

Expected outcome(s): _____

_____

Skills needed: _____

_____

Time required: _____

Deadline_____

Employee Selection

Abilities, skills, and interests:_____

_____

Time available: _____

What does the employee get out of this (motivation)?: _____

_____

Instruction or training needed: _____

_____

Communication and Follow-up

Authority delegated: _____

Responsibilities of each party:

    Delegatee: _____

    _____

    Delegator_____

    _____

Communications:

    From delegator (offer, evaluations): _____

    _____

    From delegatee (acceptance, progress and final reports): _____

    _____

Other communications (colleague reports, evaluations): _____

_____

Adapted from Ferner, 166.

Action Plan

Task or Goal	Resources (Money, People, Things)	Time Frame			
		Start Date	Milestone 1	Milestone 2	Finish
1.					
2.					
3.					
4.					
5.					
6.					
7.					
8.					
9.					
10.					
11.					
12.					
13.					
14.					
15.					

Adapted from Ferner, 243.

Appendix B

Other Examples of Time Logs

Time	Activity	Where?	With Whom?	Doing Anything Else?

Nauman, 43.

Daily Log

Time	Activity	Time Used	Priority	Comments

Daily Summary

Estimated Time	Activity	Time Used	Priority	Comments
Actual Time	**Activity**	**Time Used**	**Priority**	**Comments**

Goal Analysis

1. What time did you start on your number one goal?_____

_____

2. Could you have started earlier? _____

_____

3. Did you complete it? If not, why? _____

_____

4. How many times were you distracted from high-priority tasks?_____

_____

5. When distracted, how fast did you recover?_____

_____

6. What was your longest period of uninterrupted time? Was it spent on a high-priority task? _____

_____

_____

Adapted from Mackenzie, 45–47.

Weekly Planning Guide

Contacts		Goals	Activities			Schedule	
Key People	Key Projects	High Priorities	Work	Meetings	Phone	a.m.	p.m.

Planned Activities for the
Week of _____, 200__

Day	a.m.	Lunch	p.m.	Out of Office
Monday				
Tuesday				
Wednesday				
Thursday				
Friday				

Daily Log

Day	Telephone	Writing	Meetings	Other
Monday				
Tuesday				
Wednesday				
Thursday				
Friday				

To Discuss with: _____ **Week of:** _____, 200__

Your Boss
Priority   *Subject*

_____   _____

         _____

_____   _____

         _____

_____   _____

         _____

Technical Services Staff
Priority   *Subject*

_____   _____

         _____

_____   _____

         _____

_____   _____

         _____

Your Assistant
Priority   *Subject*

_____   _____

         _____

_____   _____

         _____

_____   _____

         _____

ILL Staff
Priority   *Subject*

_____   _____

         _____

_____   _____

         _____

_____   _____

         _____

Reference Librarian(s)
Priority   *Subject*

_____   _____

         _____

_____   _____

         _____

_____   _____

Circulation Staff
Priority   *Subject*

_____   _____

         _____

_____   _____

         _____

_____   _____

Adapted from Mackenzie, 84-85.

Sample Time Recording Form
Day: _____

Time	Quick Reference	Phone	Circula-tion	Online and WWW	House-keeping	In-House Meeting	Outside Meeting	Profes-sional Activities	Personal	Other
Day's Total										

Sample Time Recording Form—Partly Filled In
Day: <u>Tuesday, 15 September</u>

Time	Quick Reference	Phone	Circula-tion	Online and WWW	House-keeping	In-House Meeting	Outside Meeting	Profes-sional Activities	Personal	Other
8:00					Open up					
8:15			Shelving							
8:30								Read journals		
9:00						Intranet Task Force				
10:30				E-mail						
11:30	John Smith									
11:45		Boss								
12:00									Lunch Husband	
1:00-1:15		Jim Doe Re OL								
1:30				Jim Doe						
Day's Total										

Developing Your Own Service Response

For each customer need, complete the following:

1. What is the need to be addressed?

   _____

   _____

2. What can the library do to meet the need?

   _____

   _____

3. How would this help the parent organization?

   _____

   _____

4. How will this service be delivered?

   _____

   _____

5. What resources will be needed: staff, collection, facilities, technology, money?

   _____

   _____

6. How will you measure the progress you have made toward meeting the need described in question 1? (What is the number of people served? How well does the service meet the needs of the people served? Other?)

   _____

   _____

   _____

Adapted from Nelson.

Bibliography

Abernathy, Donna J. (1999). "A Get-Real Guide to Time Management." *Training and Development*, June, 53(5):22–26.

Adams, Scott. (1996). *The Dilbert Principle: A Cubicle's-Eye-View of Bosses, Meetings, Management Fads and Other Workplace Afflictions*. New York, N.Y.: HarperCollins, ISBN 0-88730-787-6.

Ainsworth, Jim. (1998). "When Time Really is Money, Delegation is Critical." *Accounting Today*, 16 March, 12(5):19–20.

Allen, Kathleen R. (1995). *Time and Information Management that Really Works!* Los Angeles, Calif.: Affinity Publishing, ISBN 0-8442-2998-9.

Allison, Michael, and Jude Kaye. (1997). *Strategic Planning for Nonprofit Organizations: A Practical Guide and Workbook*. New York, N.Y.: John Wiley, (*http://search.genie.org*; accessed 28 May 2001).

Anders, George. (2000). "Boss Talk: Taming the Out-of-Control In-Box." *Wall Street Journal*, 4 February, B1. Interview with Jeff Bezos of Amazon.com.

Aslett, Don, and Carol Cartaino. (1997). *Keeping Work Simple: 500 Tips, Rules, and Tools*. Pownal, Vt.: Store Communications, ISBN 0-88266-996-6.

Bacon, Pamela. (2000). "Quit Playing Catch-Up: A Veteran Librarian Offers Tips for Conquering a Never-Ending Job." *School Library Journal*, June 46(6):35.

Baker, Daniel L. (2001). "A Flexible and Dynamic Strategic Plan for 2001 and Beyond" [President's Memo]. *Concrete International*, July, 23(7):7.

Barclay, Laurie. (2001). "Sick of Being Boss? For Some, Taking Charge May Lead to Illness." WebMDHealth, (*http://my.webmd.com/content/article/1728.788.77*; accessed 5 May).

Bausch, Donna. (2001). "Has It Really Been That Long? A New Role Can Be Energizing," pp. 540-544. In "Care and Maintenance of the Successful Career: How Experienced Law Librarians Make Their Work Rewarding," by Paul George, *Law Library Journal*, Fall, 93(4): 535-587.

Beam, Cris. (2001). "Stop Procrastinating." *Woman's Day*, September, 64(4):1.

Beckwith, Harry. (1997). *Selling the Invisible: A Field Guide to Modern Marketing*. New York, N.Y.: Warner Books, ISBN 0-446-52094-2.

Bergonzi, Chris. (1997). "Autocrats Anonymous: It's Okay to Make a Decision, Really." *Continental* [Airlines Magazine], November, 1(8):26–27.

Berkman, Bob. (2001). "Focusing Your Attention on Information Overload." *Information Adviser*, September, 13(9):6–7.

Bernacki, Ed. (2001). "Wow! What a Great Idea! How to Find More Great Ideas at Your Next Conference!" *inCite*, August, 22(7):20.

Berner, Andrew J. (1997). "Overcoming Procrastination: A Practical Approach." *Information Outlook*, December, 1(12):23–26.

Bezos, Jeff. (2000). "5 Lessons from Amazon.com's Jeff Bezos." *CIO*, 16 June, 13(17):54.

Bly, Robert W. (1999). *101 Ways to Make Every Second Count: Time Management Tips and Techniques for More Success with Less Stress*. Franklin Lakes, N.J.: Career Press, ISBN 1-56414-406-2.

Bond, William J. (1991). *199 Time-Waster Situations and How to Avoid Them: Learn How to Manage Your Time Wisely*. Hollywood, Fla.: Fell Publishers, ISBN 0-8119-0036-3.

Boorstein, Sylvia. (1996). *Don't Just Do Something, Sit There: A Mindful Retreat*. New York, N.Y.: Harper SanFrancisco, ISBN 0-06-061252-5. This guide to a three-day meditative retreat contains some good stress reducers.

Breier, Mark, with Armin A. Brott. (2000). *The 10-Second Internet Man@ger: Survive, Thrive and Drive Your Company in the Information Age*. New York, N.Y.: Crown Business, ISBN 0-609-60732-4. See their Web site at (*http://www.10secondmanager.com*).

Bremer, Suzanne W. (1994). *Long Range Planning: A How-To-Do-It Manual for Public Librarians*. New York, N.Y.: Neal-Schuman, ISBN 1-55570-162-0.

Bruno, Frank J. (1997). *Stop Procrastination: Understand Why You Procrastinate—and Kick the Habit Forever*. New York, N.Y.: Macmillan, ISBN 0-02-861302-3.

Caldwell, Bruce. (1996). "The new outsourcing partnership." *Information Week*, (585):50.

Caputo, Janette S. (1984). *The Assertive Librarian*. Phoenix, Ariz.: Oryx, ISBN 0-89774-085-8.

Carlson, Richard. (1998). *Don't Sweat the Small Stuff at Work: Simple Ways to Minimize Stress and Conflict While Bringing Out the Best in Yourself and Others*. New York, N.Y.: Hyperion, ISBN 0-7868-8336-7.

Carlson, Richard, and Joseph Bailey. (1998). *Slowing Down to the Speed of Life*. New York, N.Y.: HarperCollins, ISBN 0-06251-454-7.

Childress, Karen. (2001). "Making Decisions Effectively," (*http:// ihavegoals.com/public/articles;* accessed 10 July).

Clark, Jonathan, and Susan Clark. (1994). *How to Make the Most of Your Workday*. Hawthorne, N.J.: Career Press, ISBN 1-56414-143-8.

Cochran, J. Wesley. (1992). *Time Management Handbook for Librarians*. Westport, Conn.: Greenwood Press, ISBN 0-313-27842-3. Good, but dated.

Cook, Marshall J. (1998). *Time Management: Proven Techniques for Making the Most of Your Valuable Time*. Holbrook, Mass.: Adams Media, ISBN 1-55850-799-X.

Cook, Rae. (2001) "Winning Over the Boss." *IEE Solutions*, January, 33(1):20–23.

Corcoran, Mary E. (1999). *Time Management for People with No Time*. Kansas City, Mo.: William Waldron, ISBN 1-893544-18-4.

Corrall, Sheila. (1994). *Strategic Planning for Library and Information Services*. London: Aslib, ISBN 0-85142-330-2.

Covey, Stephen R. (1989). *The 7 Habits of Highly Effective People* (Miniature edition). Philadelphia, Pa.: Running Press, ISBN 0-7624-0833-2.

Crouch, Clark E. (2001). "The Terminology of Strategic Planning," (*http://www.owt.com/croouch/plandef.html*; accessed 20 May).

———. (2001). "A New, Simplified Model for Planning," (*http://www.owt.com/crouch/planning.html*; accessed 20 May).

Davidson, Jeff. (1999). *The Complete Idiot's Guide® to Managing Stress*, 2nd ed. New York, N.Y.: Alpha Books, ISBN 0-02-862955-8.

———. (1999). *The Complete Idiot's Guide® to Managing Your Time*, 2nd ed. New York, N.Y.: Alpha Books, ISBN 0-02-862943-4.

———. (2000). *10 Minute Guide to Managing Your Time*. Indianapolis, Ind.: Alpha Books, ISBN 0-02-863886-7.

de Stricker, Ulla. (1998). "Marketing with a Capital S: Strategic Planning for Knowledge Based Services." *Information Outlook*, February, 2(2):28–32.

Eisenberg, Ronni, with Kate Kelly. (1997). *The Overwhelmed Person's Guide to Time Management: The Ultimate Guide to Giving Yourself More Time for Everything!* New York, N.Y.: Penguin Books, ISBN 0-452-27682-9. Contains mostly tips for you at home, but some good ideas are presented.

Ellis, Albert, and Robert A. Harper. (1975). *A New Guide to Rational Living.* North Hollywood, Calif.: Wilshire Book Company, ISBN 0-13-614909-X.

Ferner, Jack D. (1995). *Successful Time Management: A Self-Teaching Guide*, 2nd ed. New York, N.Y.: John Wiley, ISBN 0-471-03392-8.

Foust, J'aimé. (2000). "Dewey Need To Be Organized? Time Management and Organization from a Librarian Who Knows Whereof She Speaks! [Part 1]." *The Book Report*, October-November, 19(2):20–23.

——. (2000). "Dewey Need To Be Organized? Time Management and Organization from a Librarian Who Knows Whereof She Speaks! [Part 2]." *The Book Report*, November-December, 19(3):23–25.

Fraley, Ruth A. (2001). "Strategic Plans and Environmental Scans." *Law Librarians in the New Millennium* (a newsletter from West Group Librarian Relations) 3(4):1–3.

Garfield, Charles. (1981). "Why Workaholics Work." *Newsweek*, 27 April.

George, Paul M. (2001). "Care and Maintenance of the Successful Career: How Experienced Law Librarians Make their Work Rewarding." *Law Library Journal*, Fall, 93(4):535–587. Twenty-three law librarians tell how they have made the most of staying in one job for a long time.

Goodale, Mark. (2001). "Boosting Morale." *Civil Engineering*, June, 71(6):85–86.

Gordon, Gil. (2001). *Turn It Off: How to Unplug from the Anytime-Anywhere Office Without Disconnecting Your Career.* New York, N.Y.: Three Rivers Press, ISBN 0-609-806971.

Gothberg, Helen M. (1991). "Time Management in Special Libraries: Research Activity." *Special Libraries*, Spring, 82:119–130.

Goulston, Mark, and Philip Goldberg. (1995). *Get Out of Your Own Way.* New York, N.Y.: Berkeley Publishing Group, ISBN 0-39951-990-4.

Graesser, Chris. (2001). "Fire Extinguishers for Librarian Burnout," pp. 559–561. In "Care and Maintenance of the Successful Career: How

Experienced Law Librarians Make Their Work Rewarding," by Paul George, *Law Library Journal*, Fall, 93(4): 535-587.

Griessman, B. Eugene. (1994). *Time Tactics of Very Successful People.* New York, N.Y.: McGraw Hill, ISBN 0-07-024644-0.

Haddock, Patricia. (2001). *The Time Management Workshop: A Trainer's Guide.* New York, N.Y.: Amacom, ISBN 0-8144-7082-3. Tells you *everything* you need to know to conduct a time management workshop, including overheads, handouts, and a complete script, however, it is oriented to personal time management, not professional.

Hazelton, Penny A. (2001). "I Am Not Bored—And Here's Why," pp. 565-567. In "Care and Maintenance of the Successful Career: How Experienced Law Librarians Make Their Work Rewarding," by Paul George, *Law Library Journal*, Fall, 93(4): 535-587.

Hemphill, Barbara, and Pamela Quinn Gibbard. (1998). "Simplify Your Workday: How to Survive—and Thrive—from Nine to Five." Pleasantville, N.Y.: *Reader's Digest*, ISBN 0-7621-0098-2.

Himmel, Ethel, and William James Wilson. (1998). *Planning for Results: A Public Library Transformation Process.* Chicago, Ill.: American Library Association. Two volumes: ISBN 0-838934-88-9 (vol. 1), ISBN 0-838934-79-X (vol. 2).

Jacob, M.E.L. (1990). *Strategic Planning: A How-To-Do-It Manual for Librarians.* New York, N.Y.: Neal-Schuman, ISBN 1-55570-074-8.

Jacobson, Alvin L., and JoAnne L. Sparks. (2001). "Creating Value: Building the Strategy-Focused Library." *Information Outlook*, September, 5(9):14-20.

Jasper, Jan. (1999). *Take Back Your Time; How to Regain Control of Work, Information, and Technology.* New York, N.Y.: St. Martin's Griffin, ISBN 0-312-24334-0.

Kearns, Kevin P. (1997). "Managing Upward: Working Effectively with Supervisors and Others in the Hierarchy." *Information Outlook*, October, 1(10):23-27.

Kennedy, Toni. (2001). "Burnout in the Workplace." *OPALessence*, January, 5(1):305.

King, James. (1998). "Scenario Planning: Powerful Tools for Thinking about Alternatives." In *Scenario Planning for Libraries*, Joan Giesecke, ed, pp. 3-17. Chicago, Ill.: American Library Association, ISBN 0-8389-3482-X.

Koch, Richard. (1998). *The 80/20 Principle: The Secret of Achieving More with Less.* New York, N.Y.: Doubleday, ISBN 0-385-49170-0.

LeBoeuf, Michael. (1979). *Working Smart: How to Accomplish More in Half the Time*. New York, N.Y.: McGraw Hill, ISBN 0-07-036949-6.

Lemberg, Paul. (2001). "How to Get Things Done: A Guide to Strategic Planning," (*http://www.lemberg.com/strategictacticalplan.html*; accessed 20 May).

Machlowitz, Marilyn. (1981). *Workaholics: Living with Them, Working with Them*. New York, N.Y.: NAL [New American Library], ISBN 0-415162-224-3.

Mackenzie, Alec. (1990). *The Time Trap*. New York, N.Y.: Amacom, ISBN 0-8144-5969-2. This book is an excellent resource.

McCuistion, Dennis. (2001). "To Plan or Not to Plan, That is Not the Issue," (*http:// www.mccuistionv.com/articles.htm*; accessed 4 July).

McGee-Cooper, Ann, with Duane Trammel. (1994). *Time Management for Unmanageable People: The Guilt-Free Way to Organize, Energize, and Maximize Your Life*. New York, N.Y.: Bantam, ISBN 0-553-37071-5.

Meredith, M.J. (2001). www.stress-counselling.co.uk, (*http://members.farmline.com/stress/management/definition.htm*; accessed 22 October).

Messmer, Max. (1998). "Delegation: Your Key to Time Management." *Business Credit*, September, 100(8):21–22. Chairman and CEO of Robert Half International.

Miodonski, Bob. (1999). "Time Management is Key to Juggling Multiple Jobs." *Contractor*, December, 5:49.

Morgan, Eric Lease. (1999). "Springboards for Strategic Planning." *Computers in Libraries*, January, 19(1):32–33.

Morgenstern, Julie. (1998). *Organizing from the Inside Out: The Foolproof System for Organizing Your Home, Your Office, and Your Life*. New York, N.Y.: Henry Holt, ISBN 0-8050-5649-1.

Morgenstern, Julie. (2000). *Time Management from the Inside Out: The Foolproof System for Taking Control of Your Schedule and Your Life*. New York, N.Y.: Henry Holt, ISBN 0-8050-6469-9.

Murphy, Dave. (2001). "Workers Can Use Anger Positively." *San Francisco Chronicle*. Reprinted in *The Plain Dealer*, Cleveland, Ohio, 28 October, p. G3, 28.

Nauman, Ann, and Marvene Dearman. (1991). *Making Every Minute Count: Time Management for Librarians*. Berkeley Heights, N.J.: Library Learning Resources, ISBN 0-931315-06-9.

Nelson, Sandra. (2001). *The NEW Planning for Results: A Streamlined Approach*. Chicago, Ill.: ALA Editions, ISBN 0-8389-3504-4, paper. Written for the Public Library Association. Very complete. Includes: The Planning Process (designing the planning process and preparing the board, the staff, and the committee; determining community vision and identifying community needs; selecting service responses and writing goals and objectives; identifying preliminary activities and determining resource requirements; writing the basic plan, obtaining approval, and communicating the results of the planning process; and allocating or reallocating resources and monitoring implementation); Public Library Service Responses; and various forms.

Nutty, Julie. (2001). "Time Management." Presentation at Annual Meeting of the American Association of Law Libraries, Minneapolis, Minn., 16–18 July.

Oncken, William, Jr., and Donald L. Wass. (1974). "Management Time: Who's Got the Monkey?" *Harvard Business Review*, November-December, 52(6):75–80. According to Stephen Covey, this is "one of the two best-selling *Harvard Business Review* articles ever," a classic.

Parkinson, C. Northcote. (1957). *Parkinson's Law and Other Studies in Administration*. Boston, Mass.: Houghton Mifflin.

Pedley, Paul. (2001). "Time Management." *The One-Person Library: A Newsletter for Librarians and Management*, June, 18(2).

Penniman, W. David. (1999). "Strategic Planning to Avoid Bottlenecks in the Age of the Internet." *Computers in Libraries*, January, 19(1):50–53.

Pollar, Odette. (1996). *365 Ways to Simplify Your Work Life: Ideas that Bring More Time, Freedom and Satisfaction to Daily Work.* Chicago, Ill.: Dearborn Financial Publishing, ISBN 0-7931-2281-3. This book has the most tips I have ever seen, in a small and compact format.

Porat, Frieda. (1980). *Creative Procrastination: Organizing Your Own Life.* New York, N.Y.: Harper & Row, ISBN 0-06-250690-0.

Potter, Ned. (1999). "Information Overload: How to Deal with Too Much Data," *ABC News*, 3 May, (*http://more.abcnews.go.com/sections/tech/loserlook/infooverload990503.html*, quoted in Nelson, 128; accessed by Nelson, 2 March, 2000).

Quint, Barbara. (1996). "Disintermediation." *Searcher*, January, 4(1):4,6.

Riggs, Donald E. (1984). *Strategic Planning for Library Managers.* Phoenix, Ariz.: Oryx Press, ISBN 0-89774-049-1.

Saunders, Rebecca M. (2000). "Assertiveness Yourself: How to Say 'No' and Mean It." *Harvard Management Communication Letter*, July, 3(7):9–11. Contains a good assertiveness quiz.

Schein, Edgar H. (1990). "Organizational Culture: The Changing Face and Place of Work." *The American Psychologist*, February, 45(2):110–111.

_____. (1992). *Organizational Culture and Leadership*, 2nd ed. San Francisco, Calif.: Jossey-Bass, ISBN 1-55542-487-2.

Schor, Juliet B. (1991). *The Overworked American: The Unexpected Decline of Leisure.* New York, N.Y.: Basic Books, ISBN 0-465-05433-1.

Shellenbarger, Sue. (2001). "Learning How to Work With the Good Stress, Live Without the Bad." [Work & Family column], *The Wall Street Journal*, 25 July, B1.

Siess, Judith A. (1997). *The Solo Librarian's Sourcebook.* Medford, N.J.: Information Today, ISBN 1-57387-032-3.

Silber, Lee. (1998). *Time Management for the Creative Person: Right-Brain Strategies for Stopping Procrastination, Getting Control of the Clock and Calendar and Freeing Up Your Time and Your Life.* New York, N.Y.: Three Rivers Press, ISBN 0-609-80090-6.

Slyhoff, Merle J. (2001). "You've Been There *How* Long?!", pp. 579–581. In "Care and Maintenance of the Successful Career: How Experienced Law Librarians Make Their Work Rewarding," by Paul George, *Law Library Journal*, Fall, 93(4): 535-587.

Smart, Doug. (2001). "The Art of Saying 'No.'" *Arthritis Today*, March-April, 15(2):46–47.

Smith, Hyrum W. (1994). *The 10 Natural Laws of Successful Time and Life Management: Proven Strategies for Increased Productivity and Inner Peace.* New York, N.Y.: Warner Books, ISBN 0-446-51741-0. From a religious (Mormon) viewpoint.

Smith, Stanley E. (1997). *The Sacred Rules of Management: How to Get Control of Your Time and Your Work.* Acton, Mass.: Vander Wyk and Burham, ISBN 0-9641089-7-6. Contains 110 rules, is easy-to-read, and is nicely organized. Excellent.

St. Clair, Guy L. (1993). "To Memo or Not to Memo?" *The One-Person Library: A Newsletter for Librarians and Management*, October, 10(1):6.

St. James, Elaine. (2001). *Simplify Your Work Life: Ways to Change the Way You Work So You Have More Time to Live.* New York, N.Y.: Hyperion, ISBN 0-7868-6683-7.

Steiner, George A. (1979). *Strategic Planning: What Every Manager Must Know.* New York, N.Y.: Free Press, ISBN 0-02-931110-1. This book is the "bible" for strategic planning; it is very detailed, with many planning models and diagrams. Written more for business, but is still useful.

Stewart, Joan. (2001). "Surviving Pesky Patrons." *Marketing Library Services*, September, 15 (6):4–5.

Stueart, Robert D. (1986). "Long-Range Planning in U.S. Public Libraries." In *Bertelsman Foundation Colloquium: Public Libraries Today and Tomorrow: Approaches to Their Goals and Management*, Horst Ernestus and Hans-Dieter Wegner, eds., Boston Spa, England: British Library Research and Development Department, ISBN 0-71233-078-X.

Stueart, Robert D., and Barbara B. Moran. (1998). *Library and Information Center Management*, 5th ed. Englewood, Colo.: Libraries Unlimited, ISBN 1-56308-593-3 (hardcover); ISBN 1-56308-594-1 (paper).

Todaro, Julie. (1999). "Dost Thou Love Life?" *Library Administration and Management*, Summer, 13(3:)132–135.

Tolpa, Caryn. (2001). "Eight Easy Ways to Keep Your Office Clutter-Free," *Staples.com*, (*http://www.staples.com/BizServices/tools/spl. clutter_free.asp;* accessed 12 May).

Tomlin, Anne C. (2001). "OPL: Practical Tips for the Solo Practitioner." *National Network*, April, 25(4):8–9.

_____. (2001). "OPL: Practical Tips for the Solo Practitioner." *National Network*, July, 26(1):20–21.

Tullier, L. Michelle. (1999). *The Complete Idiot's Guide® to Overcoming Procrastination*. Indianapolis, Ind.: Macmillan, ISBN 0-02863637-6.

Turner, Anne Marie. (2001). "Organizing from the Inside Out." Online Course, Barnes and Noble University, September.

Veaner, Allen B. (1989). *Academic Librarianship in a Transformational Age*. New York, N.Y.: Macmillan, ISBN 0-81611-866-3.

Walster, Dian. (1993). *Managing Time: A How-To-Do-It Manual for Librarians*. New York, N.Y.: Neal-Schuman, ISBN 1-55570-127-2. This book is designed for school librarians

Watkins, Denise. (1999). "Are You a Time Management Junkie?" *Information Outlook*, January, 3(1):34–35.

Weeks, M.J. (1998). *Taking Control with Time Management*, 4th ed. New York, N.Y.: American Management Association. This self-study course is very good.

Weil, Michelle M., and Larry D. Rosen. (1998). *TechnoStress: Coping with Technology @WORK@HOME@PLAY*. New York, N.Y.: John Wiley, ISBN 0-47117-709-1.

Weisberg, Jacob. (1998). "A Time-Management Survival Guide." *Folio: The Magazine for Magazine Management*, October, 27(14):85,87.

Wells, Stuart, (2001). "To Plan, Perchance, To Think: Aye, There's the Rub," *Information Outlook*, September, 5(9):8–12.

White, Herbert S. (1990). "Librarian Burnout." *Library Journal* 115(5):65.

———. (1997). "Planning and Evaluation: The Endless Carousel." *Library Journal*, 15 November, 122, (19):38–39.

_____. (1989). "How to Cope with an Incompetent Supervisor," In *Librarians and the Awakening from Innocence: A Collection of Papers,* Boston, Mass.: G.K. Hall, pp. 213–221. Originally published in *Canadian Library Journal*, December 1987, 44:381–384.

Williams, Paul B. (1996). *Getting a Project Done on Time: Managing People, Time, and Results.* New York, N.Y.: Amacom, ISBN 0-8144-0284-4.

Willmore, Joe. (2001). "Scenario Planning: Creating Strategy for Uncertain Times." *Information Outlook*, September, 5(9):22–27.

Winston, Stephanie. (2001). *The Organized Executive: The Classic Program for Productivity: New Ways to Manage Time, Paper, People, and the Digital Office. Revised and Updated for the Digital Age.* New York, N.Y.: Warner Business Books, ISBN 0-446-676696-9.

Wood, Debra. (2001). "Surviving 'Techno-Stress.'" *Kiwanis*, August, 86(7):48–50.

Wood, Lamont. (1998). "Get Organized Now: Time Management Can Simplify Your Life." *Hispanic Business*, October, 20(9):24,26.

Index

About the Author

Judith A. Siess is a recognized expert in one-person librarianship and interpersonal networking. Judith is the author of two books, *The SOLO Librarian's Sourcebook* (1997) and *The OPL Sourcebook* (2001) and is working on a fourth book concerning advocacy and marketing for librarians. Judith received her M.S. in library and information science from the University of Illinois at Urbana-Champaign in 1982. She is active in the Special Libraries Association (SLA) and is also a member of many other worldwide library associations. She was the first chair of the Solo Librarians Division of the SLA and founded the Agricultural Economics Reference Organization in 1982. Judith was a member of the first People-to-People Citizen Ambassador delegation on information management and special librarianship to the Republic of South Africa in 1996.